1

⊤⫽⩘⫽ ⊼⫽⊂∪⋏ ⫽⩏∪⋇⫽⋇⩗⩗

This is my prayer

⨯⫽⩗⊤∨⋇⫽⊂⫽ ⨯⫽∧∧⩗⊤⋇∨; ⨯⫽⫽ ⋇⫽⊂∪4⩋⨍ ⩏⫽⪺⊓⨯⫽⫽⋇ ⩏⩋⊂ ⩗⊂
⨯⫽ᒪ∪⪺⩋⊼ ⊑∧; ⊤⫽⩘⫽ ⊼⫽⊂∪⋏ ⫽⩏∪⋇⫽⋇⩗⩗ ⫽∧⫽∪∧⩗⩗ ⩗⊂
4⫽⨉∪⊂◌ ⊂⩋⊤⊤⫽ ⨯⫽⩏⫽⋏ ⊼⫽⪺ ⊤⫽⩘⫽ ⩏⫽⫽⩏⊂; ⫽∧∪⊼⩋ ⫽⊤∪⊓ⱹⱹ⊼⨳
⊼⫽⪺ ⫽⩏∪⊤⩗⩗; ⨯⨯⫽4∪⋇⩗⩗ ⊼⫽⊂∪⋏ ⩋⫽⫽⨉∪ⱻ ⨳⩋⋏, ⊂⫽⊼∪⋏ ∧∪⊼
⩏⫽⩏∪⊂.

4⫽⋏ ⨯⨯⫽4∪⋇⫽⫽⋇ ⫽∧∪⊼⩋ ⊼⫽ⱹ⩋∧∪⋇ ∧⫽⫽∪∧⩗⩗ ⩗⊂ 4⫽⨉∪⊂◌,
⩗⊂ ⊤⫽⊼∪⨳⊓∪⨳, ⨯⨯⫽ ⩗⊂ ⱹ⫽∧∪⩋ ⊂⩋⊤⊤⫽ ⫽⫽⫽∪⩋ ⩗⊂ ⋇⫽⪺∪4
⊼⫽◌⫽⊂⩗⊼ ⊓⩗⊼ ⫽∧⋇∪⩋ ⩏⫽⊼∪⊂ ⨯⫽ⱹ∪⊼ ⩗⊂ ⨯⨯⫽4∪⫽
⫽⊂⫽.

⊂⩋ ⫽⊂⫽⫽⫽⋇ ⩏⩋ ⱹ⫽∧∪⫽⫽⋇ ⩗∧⩗∧ ⊼⫽⩋∪⋇ ⫽-⋇⫽⊤⫽⩋ ⊂⩋
⊤⫽⩘⫽ ⨯⨯⫽4∪⋇.

⊂⩋ ⊤⫽⩘⫽ ⨯⨯⫽4∪⋇.

⫽∧∪⊼⩋ ⫽⫽ ⊤⫽⨉∪⊓⨳∪⊂ ⊂⩋⊤⊤⫽ ⊼∪⩋∨⋇⫽ ⫽⋇-∪4⊂∨⋏ ⫽⨳⨳⫽
⨯⨯⫽⊤∨⊓ ⩏⩋⊂ ᒪ⫽⩋∪⋇-∪⊼, ⨯⨯⫽ ∧∪⊼ ⱹ∨⫽⫽ ⊓⫽⨉∪⨳ ⫽⊂⫽.
⊤⫽⩘⫽ ⩏⫽⊼∪⊂ ⊼⫽⊂∪⋏ ◌⫽4∪⋇.

2

Oh, Giver of Breath, oh creative forces of the galactic universe this is my prayer. Give me the strength to continue with this work. I am lonesome with my pain; my time is running out, but I work. Sometimes I am fragile give me the strength, the wisdom, and the patience to prepare the path well that they can carry the job on. For thousands of years, we have waited for this time. For this time, I am so grateful to have been chosen as your one of slave, and I will carry on. This can be trusted.

Black-Hawk H. Thunderbird
Sage RaMus

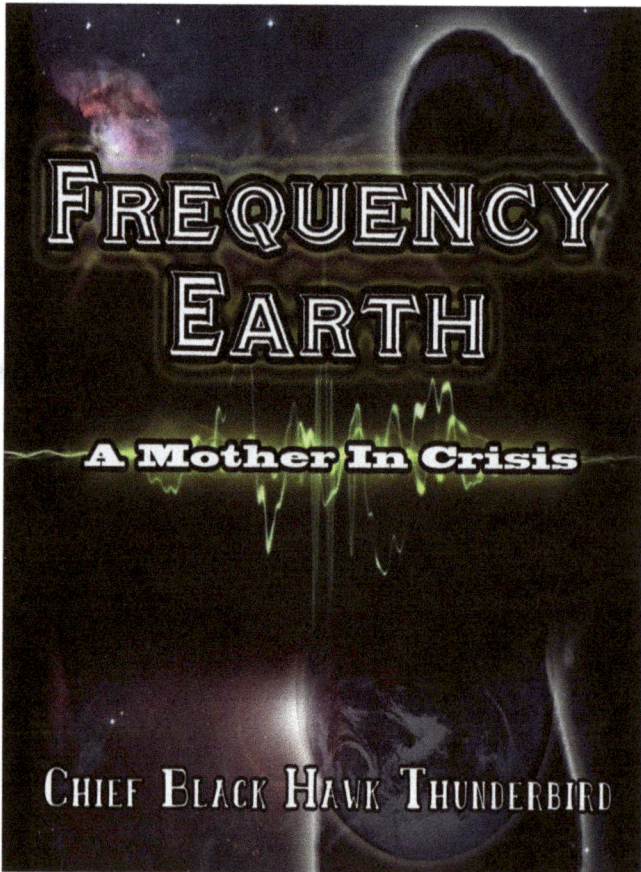

FREQUENCY EARTH

A Mother In Crisis

CHIEF BLACK HAWK THUNDERBIRD

Frequency Earth: A Mother in Crises

MOTHER EARTH IS SICK AND THIS SICKNESS SHOULD BE CURED!!!

US Copyright © 2012, 2021 by S.G. Chief Black Hawk H. Thunderbird

ROYAL THUNDERBIRD INTERPRIZES in Association with RaMus publishing

INARS catalog number: 001-00100109

ISBN 978-1-7358970-2-8

This is not what one might call a typical religious work, and the assessments are not different from the teachings of the masters of any of the major religions. We make no distinction as to an individuals' faith. Our faith is Reflective Human Socialization. Our gratitude is the "The Great Spirit Giver of Breath, the Creative Forces of the Galactic Universes." *Sage Ramus*

A single thought has risen that demands liberation and a world "crucified" of its cross of ignorance, of poverty, of subjection, and of dependence to build a resurrected world, that is to say to build a world where humans are worthy of life.

Saqur/Popocatzin

Istartaal Hayuh "El janub Nasfa Kara Thaguf"

Recitation Life "The Sothern Culture"

We are pure energy, a single thought manifesting with a double movement in the cosmos. We are kin to the ethers, the fire, the air, the wind, the water, and Mother Earth.

We are conceived within the cycles of time within this Universe. With the turn of time we manifest, brought through by the nature of and for this planet. Our essence has grown from the water and soil of "Earth" our Mother.

Our essence is shared among many, stemming from the branches of a great tree that sprang forth from this land. Our branches extend, and our foliage continues to spread like a canopy across this Land now called America. We are called "The Southern "Cult". We are "Indigenous".

Black-Hawk Hommie. Thunderbird
Sage RaMus

Contents

PRELUDE...11

PART 1 ~ 20

What is REFLECTIVE HUMAN
SOCIALIZATION/Reflective Humanism 20

    INTRODUCTION TO CYMATICS...............................25

    DNA EXPLOSIONS 31

    ELECTROMAGNETIC FREQUENCIES.......................38

    MOTHER EARTH RENEWED.......................................45

PART 2 ~ 48

UNIVERSAL LIFE & LIFE FORMS 48

    REFLECTIVE HUMANISM SOCIALIZATION IN
    ACTION 53

    THE LEGEND OF THE EAGLE AND THE SNAKE 56

    ENERGETIC COEXISTENCE.......................................60

    CONVERSATIONS..64

    A LIVING ORGANISM...73

    RECLAIMING THE LAND...77

    THE SUNS 85

PART 4 ~ 88

THE POLITICS OF CURING MOTHER EARTH 88

    INDIGENOUS SELF-DETERMINATION 96

LAWS OF NATIONALITY... 111

LINEAGE TO THE LAND 115

THE MBC-INAAN CONSTITUTION & FAQ 118

CONCLUSION.. 147

PRELUDE

To live or to die, that is the question

THE GREAT QUANTUM JUMP

Now we will give you a treatment, this is strong medicine.

This is strong medicine. This which I give to you, is for the essence of your being. I speak to you now as a Grand Master, a Sage of our Clan.

It is a great honor and a privilege for me to be chosen to share this information with you. As Most Principal Chief and a Sage among the MBC/INAAN of North America, it is my responsibility to comprehend and teach our people of the plight of our Mother Earth and her children to the best of my ability. What am I to you? I am "Gesur" Aswud Sagr Hommie Saqur, that is to say Most Principal Chief "Black-Hawk Hommie Thunderbird", Most Principal Chief of the Mund Bareefan Shagruth Gabelu.

About the Author:

My father was the late Honorable "Hommie Sanders Jr."; son of "Hommie Sanders Sr." and "Annis Hae Sanders", both Hommie Sr. and Annis Hae were descendants of freed Native American Slaves residing in the **Allendale Barnwell Yamassee** region of the **South Carolina territory**.

> "Among the other Black nations who existed in the Americas before Columbus and long before Christ were the Jamassee (Yamassee), who had a large kingdom in the southeastern United States. Their descendants were among **the first Blacks of pre-Columbian_American origins who fell victim to kidnapping for the purpose of enslavement. Blacks of South America, the Caribbean and Central America were also attacked and enslaved** based on a Pontifax passed during the mid- 1400's by the Church hierarchy giving the Europeans the go

ahead to enslave all "Children of Ham" found in the newly discovered territories. **The descendants of the Jamassee are the millions of Blacks who live in Alabama, Georgia, South Carolina and northern Florida**".

Online writer Paul Barton

My indigenous designation is Guale-Yamassee. Guale was also the name of the US State now called Georgia. For the record, Derrick Hommie Sanders is the name my parents gave me at birth.

My mother was the Honorable Viola Allen Sanders daughter of Irvin Allen and Viola Ben Allen, also from the **Allendale Barnwell Yamassee** region of the **South Carolina territory**. Viola Ben's tribal name was "Minnie". "Minnie's" grandmother was an indigenous individual from Alabama. Her husband was English and was tarred and feathered for being married to her. She escaped and migrated to Georgia as a free woman of means and became a slave owner, her descendants would eventually become slaves, then married into the Allen's and the Sanders of South Carolina. Our family resides in many if not all the Southeastern States, historically. We are of Muscogee linguistic stock, of the "Southern Cult".

I am a college graduate of Northeastern Christian University. and have earned an Associate of Science, with concentrations in music, science, and religion of course. I worked with the Government of the Commonwealth of Pennsylvania Department of Public Welfare Region 3, as the Executive Administrator of a Sensitivity Awareness Training Program from 1973 through 1978. The Pennsylvania Department of Public Welfare Region 3 was under the direction of "Deputy Secretary" Don Jose Stovall in those years.

In 1978 I returned to faith based issued, finished my undergraduate classes at the Ansar Allah Community's University of Islaam, where I received a Ph.D. in Religious Studies worked as a Senior Minister and Professor. In 2004, along with my wife, Red SylverFox, and our son RedTail Hawk established the MBC/INAAN Department of Education for our family and other indigenous peoples of the southeast, and through-out America. . I have also had sittings with elders and chief of other clans. The Guale, Yamassee, are part of the Aninunweyan (We the People) society. The Guale, Yamassee, the Creek, the Cherokee, Black feet clans, and many others are one. We are all family.

Among our Islamic brethren I am called "Imir Abdul-Latiyf Abdullah Muhammad", **Imir**, Prince of the inner house, **"Abdul-Latiyf,"** Servant of the most Subtle One, **"Abdullah,"** Servant of Allah **"Muhammad,"** One who is worthy of praise. I have reached the highest ranks among "The Ancient and Mystic Order Melchizedek" carrying the designation" **Nayya Latuf El**", The Nobel Kind One. Among our Egyptian and brethren of the Om, I am called **RaMus Mery Amun**. RaMus **"Re/Ra**, has **Chosen** him"; and I have been **chosen** by the evolution of time and nature for this mission. **Mery "Beloved"**, **Amun- "Hidden One"**. I have been purposely **hidden** not in the background but among you; operating **in plain sight** for this mission. If you were part of the Yamassee Union of TaMa Re, this designation as your Chief, a great yet difficult responsibility was placed upon me for you the by the great one himself. **Don't believe me. Check it out for yourself.** The name I am call that brings great smiles to my heart is **ABU**, it means **Father.**

I have studied as a student of especially important people. The most impactful in my life are:

My Mother, Viola Allen Sanders who never let us her children forget that we her family are indigenous.

"Rev. William L. Bentley", founder of the Black Clergyman Council and Emmanuel Institutional Baptist Church in Philadelphia Pennsylvania; home of what he coined Practical Religion.

"Brigadier William Dearin Sr." this man became the inspiration of my education.

My Imam, Imam Isa of the Ansar Allah Community.

El Qubt (The Axis) of The Ancient and Mystic Order Melchizedek.

Chief Black Thunderbird Eagle"   Chief of the Yamassee union on TaMa Re.

Most recently I was invited and recognized to sit among the Brotherhood of the Great Spirit, Creative Forces of the Galactic Universe. They sent their representative... Tlamatinime Cuaupopocatzin "lord of the Voice." He is called the Mexican Tehuti. He was sent to us as the messenger for 200 clans and tribes of north America.

To **my indigenous family** members. **I am Black-Hawk your brother**. I am a long standing elder in the family. To some of you I am father, father-in-law, I am grandfather to some and great grandfather and uncle to others (y)our children.

If you are of Ta Ma Re, Chief Black Thunderbird Eagle himself appointed me a Chief amongst the Yamassee in 1995 upon the original charter of our family mission. We re-located back to the southeast, from Philadelphia Pennsylvania to Eatonton Georgia in April 1997 and began our work. Then in 2003 Chief Black Thunderbird Eagle requested and acknowledged me as "interim Chief for his Clan". **Don't believe me. Check it out.**

I am chosen to lead MBC/INAAN and any other member of our family who still wish to declare their Native American identity on paper as associated with the MBC/INAAN. We know of and respect every one's right to her/his right to **self-determination**. We welcome all, come and sit with us.

I have not assumed these positions and titles as I have just informed you. Among with our Clan I, have been chosen and acknowledged. Firstly, by Hotala Manneyto, "The Giver of Breath" Imam Isa, El Qubt, and by my mentor and friend Grand Chief Black Thunderbird Eagle. And, once again I/we received the acknowledgements of Chiefs and Sages of over 200 clans/tribes in 29,000 towns of indigenous populations in Central and North America by Tlamatinime Cuaupopocatzin "Lord of The Voice" , my friend and companion.

I am the product of more than seventy years of twisting, instruction, and programming; of DNA/genetic engineering and grooming by the hands of the "Mother Earth" and by the teachings Masters of the Great Spirit, Creative Forces of the Galactic Universe".

PART 1 ~

What is REFLECTIVE HUMAN SOCIALIZATION/Reflective Humanism

Humans on this continent and all around the world had developed societies, clans, tribes, and alliances. Our ancestors lived in systems that were based in abilities granted to humans by "Father Sky" and "Mother Earth" as time moves forward we are blessed with wise elders, and spiritual leaders supported by the written experiences from the Prophets, Sages, and many other Clerics who assist us with the development of well balanced, harmonious societies, which are based in human intellect called "Reflective Humanism".

Indigenous peoples around the world have always used what we described as "Reflective Human Socialization" also called "Reflective Humanism", as the means to set our moral and ethical standards and to develop and govern our environments.

Reflective Humanism: Unlike with the anthropocentric paradigm central to most governments and religions of today, Reflective Humanism, lived by indigenous people for centuries is directed by "human intellect", from the collective, not from the top down or from some individual sovereign entity. We honor and are grateful to all of the Masters, our spiritual ancestors, and honor their teachings and guidance.

Jointly, we exist as indigenous peoples we are". We lay claim, that we are indigenous peoples with personal, historical, State, and US Federal Acknowledgement of our birth rights as the indigenous peoples we are. (For more about Reflective Humanism see Reflective Human Socialization & Governance in the 21st century for Indigenous & Aboriginal Peoples. ISBN # 978-0-9857375-6-6)

THE GEOGRAPHICAL POSITION OF MU

Within the genetic structure of sentient beings are allies from over 100,000 years of information of sentient history **on this planet Earth**; starting with two of the most ancient civilizations on Earth, Mu-Lemuria, and Atlantis.

Being a "Sage"

Being a "Sage" is not that we have our minds saturated with information or that the sages are full of knowledge. The sage's true wisdom consists of being able to be happy in its world. Wisdom consists in the sage's abilities to be competent and at peace within one's own reality. That is just how it is with your interior peace. Being a sage is the product of the acceptance of that world where there is no election, or where there are not too many chaotic perspectives, but you choose that which you say you want to see, the interior peace; and you learn how to be appreciative of what you already have. When we impose too many emotional and personal perspectives, we tend to judge things as good, or bad. When we judge situations as good or bad, we confuse reality with our subjective interpretation of situations, and we are filled with mental conflicts.

This is called the law/principle of "conflicting correspondence" which leads to being mentally conflicted or to mental confusion. Being mentally and emotionally conflicted is the experience that the external world offers us. We must learn to connect with the inner being in peace to battle with the mental conflicts.

Regarding faith-based religious initiatives, this work is not to challenge your personal faith. As to faith, we say hold on to your faith!

> "Hold on to what is good even if it is a handful of earth. Hold on to your faith even if   it is a tree which stands by itself. Hold on to what you must do

even if it is a long way from here. Hold on to life even when it is easier letting go. Hold on to my hand even when I have gone away from you."

~Indigenous traditional

INTRODUCTION TO CYMATICS

Now we will discuss a new science called Cymatics. Cymatics is the science of the relationship that all living beings shear with our mother "Earth". This is not Metaphysics; this lesson is about the working of our mother Earth at the Quantum level. This is about the Quantum Mechanics of "Earth".

You are about to learn that science has caught up with what has been traditionally called stories of the ancients, or stories of man's aura and spiritual energy waves. Now that the scientific world has instruments that can measure this energy their science is called Cymatics.

Doctor Hans Jenny, doctor, and Swiss scientist with help from his colleagues studied the relationships between physical things and energy, his research is supported very well by methods that are documented and that can be reproduced in laboratories. With his research he built the foundation of their new science. It took Doctor Jenny fourteen years of experimentation to check that the quantum, cellular, evolutionary, and physical complexity of adult or smaller grade beings, depends on the energy frequencies that our bodies receive over time.

Knowing this and with a posture of deep observation (by focusing our thoughts) you will be able to comprehend that we are part of vibration frequencies that take place in physical things called dimensions. To human conciseness, dimensions are designs that may seem peculiar. Humans experience dimension at quantum levels which are not usually experienced as a part of physical reality, so their reality seems peculiar to humans. However, as Mother Earth's frequency change, the physical body mutation of living beings will be changing in matching or similar form. In this day in time because of humans, the frequencies have become irregular. Let us list some of the effects of irregular frequency changes that are happening with life on Mother Earth as the consequences of the irregular frequency changes caused by humans and other sentient beings:

- There is an alteration in the balance of the Planet.
- There is loss of Mother Earth's gravitational stability and.
- There is acceleration of the planetary turn.
- There are more and more occasions of Mother Earth being bombarded with energies of high frequency coming from the sun central galaxy, the frequencies are penetrating Mother Earths ionosphere because of the lack of internal defenses of the electromagnetic system of the planet and her children.

With the current time accelerations at times, it seems that one day today is equal to 16 hours and the four cardinal directions are not four but now at six. The four stations are: north, east, south, west, and do not forget we have magnetic north, and magnetic south. What could all this mean for Earth, Humans, and other life forms on Earth?

These are just some of the immediate effects that are presented to earth and to humans due to these electromagnetic changes. Have you noticed that the time seems to move more quickly every day? If your answer is yes, it is not you alone that finds the time seems to lapse quicker and the day no longer seems to have the 24 hours that the clock points out, and time seems to be out of sorts. What has lost temper is the pulse of the ionosphere in the skies. The ionosphere was depleted in the 20th Century because man's use of floral hydrocarbons in household and industrial aerosol spray products. The pulse has changed from 7.83 hertz to much faster vibrations. Some scientists say Mother Earth is now at 12 hertz and that there seems to be moments that Mother Earth has just16 hours in a day, altering the whole electrical system of earth and the balance of all her living beings. Some humans are feeling what the scientists' calculations now indicate. Some humans seem to be oblivious to this or are confused by this. Why? Because the managers of time (the clocks) continue the same old-time schedules that are calculated in relation to the circumference of Mother Earth, which remains unchanged at 24,000 kilometers.

Know this, it is not Mother Earth's millage. It is Mother Earth's pulse that determines the true dimension of time that we live in, or what humans perceive as time. Why? Mother Earth's pulse corresponds to the heart pulse of living beings, it is also that which affects the circadian circles, "also called the Alpha region" of the brain. It is Mother Earth's pulse that accelerates the electrical rhythm of the entire cellular system of all living beings including trees, bushes, small plants, insects, birds, land and water animals, and humans. Because of our connection to Mother Earth's pulse our cells accelerate their pulse to adapt to the increment of the pulse of Mother. Our perception of time depends on the speed of Mother Earths' pulse.

An un-restrain-able dimensional change

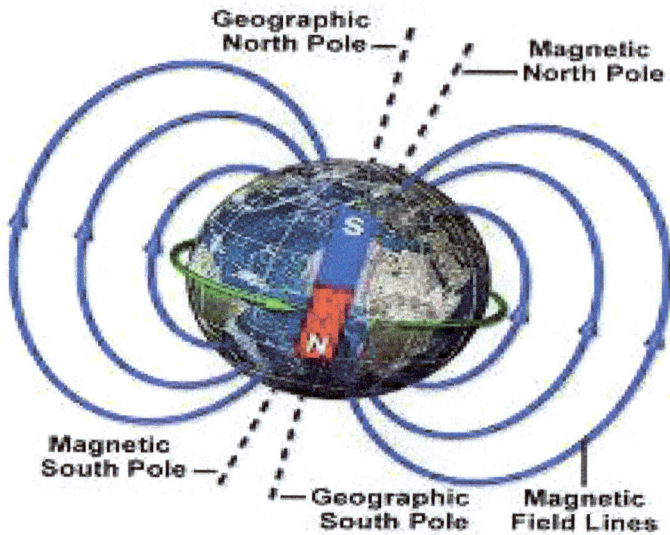

An un-restrain-able dimensional change is manifesting for Earth and living beings. Earth's rhythmic resonance which was set at 7.83 hertz is changing. The pulse is rising and may stop when it arrives at 13 hertz and it will be then, when arriving at that threshold, the surviving humans will stabilize in an eighth superior frequency and life will begin another stage of creation, in a different reality designed for humans. How? Thru the process of biological explosions or biological expansions in our "DNA".

DNA EXPLOSIONS

To Humans, the interpretation of reality has been firmly anchored in the third dimension, with only the capacity of perceiving a very narrow fringe of the creation codes that fluctuates in the spectrum among the electromagnetic frequencies higher than infra-red light, and below ultra-violet light. For that reason, our brain which works like a resonance box, has activated only 10% of its capacity at a time; while the remaining 90% of its possibilities sleeps because it corresponds to frequencies of other dimensions of light energy that we are just now being tuned to experience.

Tuning the brane to the new electromagnetic energies calls for a well-balanced brain.

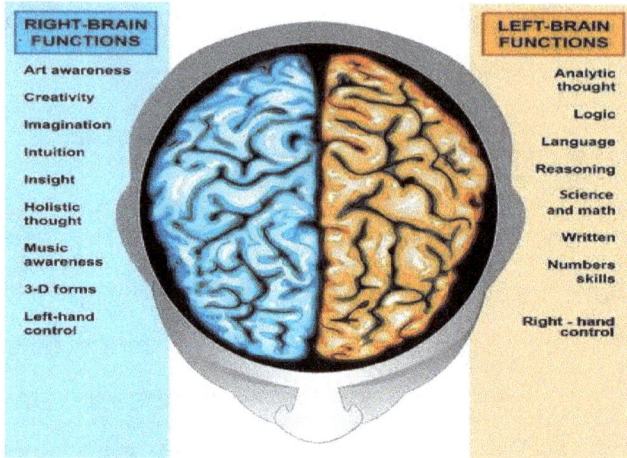

RIGHT-BRAIN FUNCTIONS	LEFT-BRAIN FUNCTIONS
Art awareness	Analytic thought
Creativity	Logic
Imagination	Language
Intuition	Reasoning
Insight	Science and math
Holistic thought	Written
Music awareness	Numbers skills
3-D forms	
Left-hand control	Right - hand control

Achieving more complete mental capacity: The are two (2) hemispheres of the human brain with different cognitive functions. It is important to know that to achieve more complete capacity, we must balance the two hemispheres of our brains, right and left. As of now most of humans' function with the left the more structured side, or the right more creative side of the brain. When we achieve the **balance**, the brain can work in harmony with itself increasing our capacity in this domain of the third dimension; giving us capacity to move forward.

*Note: Our Surgeon General "Sacred Feather Eagle" known to many of you as Dr. Jewel Pookrum MD. Is our specialist with Brane Balancing and has made... I recommend that you visit her webpage for more information on Braine Balancing. Contact: https://www.juis.education/courses/djbp/ and visit:

> The *J.E.W.E.L. Univ. of Immortal Sciences for Immortal Living. I. The College of Immortal Sciences, II. The College of Neurosciences, III. The College of Earth and Botanical Sciences, IV College of Quantum Physics for the Human Avatar, V. College of Immortal Architecture, VI. College of Geometry and Binary Mathematics, VII. College of TIME sciences and TIME as Art management VIII. School of Quantum Nutrition IX. College of Hygiene X. School of Social and Cultural Architecture, XI. College of Medical Anthropology, XII College of Astronomy, XIII College of Light & Melanin and Light-Melanin research.*

What happens to us when our cells receive the current electromagnetic frequencies from the Sun, and what is the purpose? The first step of the change is in the cells toward the 'old electric energy code information' which is or shall have become outdated information. The outdated information is rendered inactive and drained. This happens because of the previous outdated information patterns must be drained of its energy before the newly replaced code information can show in our DNA. In the following step the newly entered codes are reorganized, producing more perfect beings as 'now' also called "time" expands. **Diet is also important.** It **may** be that you are of those concerned ones because your energy operates with many ups and downs, sometimes throwing into a state of intense fatigue, or if you oscillate emotionally between depression and euphoria. **You may think** you are, **but you may not** be a bipolar psychopath. Check with your Doctor.

How does this DNA thing work? What is the process?
It is the same as when you tune an old radio. You must move forward and backward on the tuner to get to the exact station. Our cells are now oscillating back and forth from one frequency to other; all being about achieving synchrony and balance that will place us in concert with the new electromagnetic frequencies of the trilogy, EARTH-ATMOSPHERE – IONOSPHERE. Humans feel the process physically and emotionally, and every time

the frequencies of the planet changes or fluctuates you fluctuate also, to more or to less. In some cases, humans young and old may be displaying irregular heart rhythms. This can happen due to the quick fall of the magnetic field of Mother Earth. How? magnetism is a stabilizing force, and the existing cellular magnetism struggles to make our heat keep its old rhythm.

To be able to assimilate the new information, the hard disk of our internal clock the brain's alfa region also needs to be off and then re-ignited by Mother Earths' pulse to re-establish our entire system with the upgraded codes. It is like when you upgrade your electronic devices, you download new files shut down the device then turn it back on. The upgrades are recognized.

The remodeling of the DNA can produce waves of fatigue and pain. There can be sharp periods when the highest frequencies impact our body followed by a softer time of assimilation. During the sharp cycle there is necessity to sleep and to rest more. It is necessary to notice that all these symptoms are temporary; they will last while Mother Earth completes her childbirth work, and with her we will go by a new birth to the fourth dimension and beyond. This point that we live in today represents the" Great Jump" of the Planet to recover its balance and to remain aligned in concert with the cosmic planetarium.

But at the same time the moment represents the great end, the point Zero, when turning off our systems then they are lit again, a more perfect Earth and more perfect humans will be born. In the moment that the magnetic field of Mother Earth reaches the point 0, alone in that event will it be possible for Earth's pulse to complete the re-configuration of all our genetic patterns, and to make them capable for life in a dimension integrated into a bigger system. Remember this,

- the frequencies in the ionosphere are exceedingly high,
- they have been changing the magnetic pulse of Mother Earth,

- they activate toward structures in each cell, and they accelerate the vibration of earth and of our cells.

Our cells react irradiating the energy of the new creation codes and heat to other cell and through the empty spaces that surround the insides of the cells. This causes an implosion within the cells. The implosion awakens some sleeping codes of the DNA and it expands the new information toward the nuclei of other activated cells. The process will have the effect on our bodies by causing a re-configuration that will expand Human consciousness that is consistent with a finer cellular material, and a supposedly more perfect form. We pray that at the end you and your offspring are among the survivors!

Conclusion: If for the time being you cannot concentrate on anything, overstand that your body is adapting to the changes of Mother Earth, and the human brain and human nervous system is under reconstruction. The best form of overstanding how the planet is assisting humans through this great jump, this **DNA expansion** into the next level, is by taking into consideration that at the molecular level the physical body contains energy waves that immediately respond to interacting frequency characteristics of our LIVING PLANET, adapting to them, thereby making changes in our **DNA patterns**. The ethical motive for all of this is the possibility to overstand the meaning of life according to a new level of perception. All of this and more is what we are referring to when we say **DNA explosions**.

ELECTROMAGNETIC FREQUENCIES

What defines the morality (ethical motive) of what human life on earth should be? Some call it the gods, some say our planet, some say it is human beings or extraterrestrial aliens. We, the Brotherhood of the Masters of the Great Spirit Creative Forces of the Galactic Universe are here to inform you that it is the Suns' electromagnetic energy that the Planet and life on the planet is enabled to integrate. The levels of electromagnetic energy that we are currently experiencing places us in the third dimension. In the third dimension we perceive that energy like two waves with different properties:

electricity and magnetism. The electric portion provides information of the creation codes, and the magnetism stabilizes them. In this form the two polarities act together to maintain this level of reality of the third dimension of: this that and these, people, places, and things; height, length, width.

Do you get it?

Look at the images on the next page.

1. One Dimensional World

a one dimensional creature would be a point.

a 2-D world has length and breadth(but no height).

3. Three Dimensional World

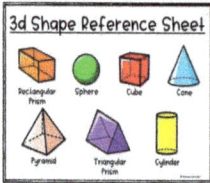

Three dimensions has the privilege of a third parameter called height. And till now the amount of universe we can observe and study is a part of the 3-D world.

4. Four Dimensional World

This is a mathematical model of a 4th Dimensional world. **It is called a Tesseract** . This is a still image and this is why it is relatively hard to figure out. You may also be a bit confused, but that is 100% okay as the figure you see is actually an attempt to depict a 4th dimensional world in a 3rd dimensional universe copied from a 2-D screen.

Let's return to our discussion on electromagnetic frequencies of light in the third dimension.

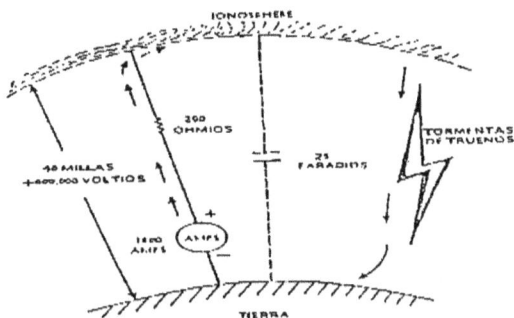

Circuito equivalente al campo de voltaje electrostático de la Tierra.

Figura 2

Electromagnetic frequencies of light take place as pulsations, and the rhythm synchronizes the cycles. Mother Earth, for example, is very vulnerable to the electromagnetic emissions of the solar explosions every eleven years, or about 9 times in a century but Mother Earth is not affected as other non-living planets. You ask Why? The magnetic loads of the Ionosphere and the cosmos are the same and therefore much of the cosmic emissions coming toward earth are repelled. Enough of the emissions does get through taking packages of new information that provoke a more complex classification at all levels from the planetary into the molecular level. With the adaptation the rising Quantum Jump, comes the opening to life and changing sense of right and wrong.

Ever Since 1987 the impact of towering frequency of photons (microscopic light beams) have been amplified upon Mother Earth, the photons are coming from the galactic center of our Sun. Up to now the Mother Earth is provided protection by the charge of the trilogy, EARTH-ATMOSPHERE – IONOSPHERE.

These three EARTH - ATMOSPHERE – IONOSPHERE execute a task similar an electric pile that contact each other to maintain a magnetic intensity of low voltage in Earths' Atmosphere. As for the water and the trees, the trees act as drivers. For that reason, the conservation of trees is important. The magnetic potential of the ionosphere due to the proper functioning of the trilogy, EARTH-ATMOSPHERE– IONOSPHERE works as a shield against the emissions of High Voltage that is coming from the cosmos.

Like Humans the trees play an especially important role in the process. There is also scientific confirmation that, perhaps due to this energy bombing Earth, some planetary constants, such as the magnetism and the pulsation of Mother Earth have been changing.

Scientist have calculated that the magnetism on Earth will have reached the point zero in this century, and the resonance bases of Mother Earth, or Schumann frequency may ascend from 7.8 to 13 Hz with the exposition of high voltage energy that could set Mother Earth on fire. Many humans though this would happen in the year 2012. We dodged that one. What could this cause to happen? A focus point that is expected to accommodate 60 electric watts could be hit with as much as 600 watts. In the critical moment that this happens, the intellect of life forms as we comprehend will disappear and the new intellectual human life forms will appear with the dimensional change that will put an end to the limitations and the lack of overstanding that human beings now demonstrate. The first movement toward establishing a new order is to the chaos of the old, outdated information. Mother Earth is also making climate changes. The elements and the geology of Earth are also shaken but, these are the change and the adjustments that allow the Planet to recover the cosmic stability that man has broken. Therefore, all the existent paradigm: at the government level, the institutions, the religions, and beliefs, the social, family systems, and of health systems, etc. is cracking to finally succumb to a more agreeable system.

MOTHER EARTH RENEWED

From April 13, of the year 2002, the new womb of creation, or energy grid was completed. Indigenous clans all over the planet began to revive ceremonies for bringing in a cyclical change. Mund Bareefan Clan completed our authentication as Indigenous people of America one year later. Some humans do not want others to know about this because they are afraid to move into the new dimension that we will be given. What some humas do not realize is that thanks to humans' destructive ways, and constant pillaging of the planet, the new information codes now flow more quickly, waking up the avenging energy that will take charge of re-establishing order. When these new energies enter Mother Earth, because of the new information the political, social, and economic systems are being affected including new geologic and climatic patterns; and its faiths and beliefs are challenged with different experiences.

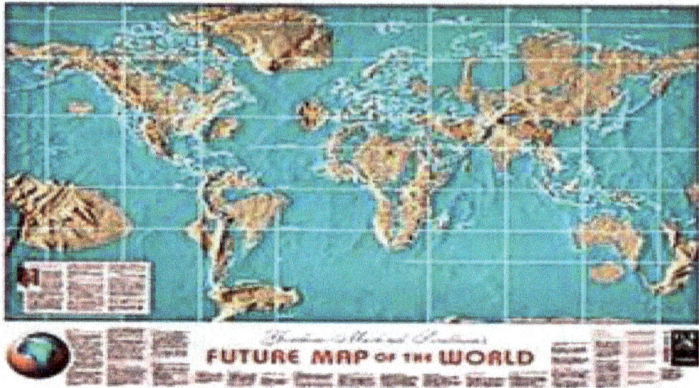

FUTURE MAP of the WORLD

All of the ancient calendars: The Vedic, Sumerian, Mayan, Tibetan, Egyptian, Chinese, etc. all coincide that, in the time that we live today a definitive change will be given in the continuity of LIFE IN AND ON MOTHER EARTH. The moment will be tragic. But it even represents that humanity has the capacity, and it indicates our opportunity to survive the changes. The predictions are not final sentences. They are information, of what can happen; and, that it should/could be avoided. **If we co-operate** the planetary in-stability is reversible, but human nonsense and **materialistic attachment** can prevent man from saving his species. **If you want to participate in this adventure beyond yourself and connect with the wave which includes the whole of**

creation, there are configuration changes that you should make. The new configuration is the action for the recovery of the electromagnetic stability that we are losing and to maintain an opening toward **"the solidify of spirit of all species"**; then to **be reconnected with our true nature like beings of light movement.** This will also serve as the access frequency to survival. Master this lesson and you will be well on your way to being counted in that number.

PART 2 ~

UNIVERSAL LIFE & LIFE FORMS

"Freedom, Justice, and Justness": This inspiring concept, this spiritual reality is one that should be felt from within indigenous concepts of REFLECTIVE HUMAN SOCIALIZATION. This spiritual reality should be sustained among the MBC/INAAN Native American Association of Nations nationals as well as with indigenous peoples at large. "Freedom, Justice, and Justness" arises naturally within the intellect of indigenous people around the globe; it is the expression of the Universe at its core. With our efforts to achieve Freedom, Justice, and Justness in the global process of man's social evolutionary history, of man's cosmic search for the total man, SECURITY, EQUALITY and SOLIDARITY possess a central place and **should be in tuned** and placed in concert with **the evolutionary process of Universal Expansion**. We say, "As above, So below".

In our effort to overstand the Universe, indigenous peoples, appeal to the category of "SPIRIT" for the overstanding of the current cosmology, and what the "Great Spirit" has in store for Earth, and life on Earth including the humans. The spirit is present in the Universe from its origin. In consequence, there is no distinction "between spirit and nature, but there are different grades of realization, and the principle "SPIRIT in Nature, and SPIRIT in Human Beings".

Yes, indigenous people have a cosmology, a spiritual plurality and a spiritual oneness as do other peoples. Some day we will speak to you of Hotala Manneyto, Manneyto, Optichi Manneyto and Ocasta. Those are ancient indigenous spiritual qualities you will learn about in other lessons.

In current societies sustained by many other humans, many especially important "Spiritual" leaders come to mind; example: three are, Master Yashua (the man called "Jesus") and "Master Mustafa" (the man called "Muhammad") both men were of the house of "Master Abraham". You may think that is not important, but it is. Why? But you should already know. In the current forms of our social existence the "story" of three two men is the same story, not three different stories. How and why? Because there is only one story that spans this timeline; and this story line has been purposely misinterpreted for centuries upon the unknowing by "Men of Knowledge".

What many of you may not know or overstand is that with both Master Yashua (the man called "Jesus") and "Master Mustafa" (the man called "Muhammad") part of their mission was to elaborate the same objectives that show man's cosmic relevance, and the interrelationships between the History of the Universe, the History of the Planet, and Human History.

Another spirit/energy I deal with is Tlamatinime Cuaupopocatzin "Lord of the Voice" also of the Galactic Brotherhood of the Great Spirit of the Galactic Universe. He came to me in the person of Dr. Raymundo Lopez Ortiz. He has explained to me that in the history of indigenous peoples our sages describe that human behavior and thought patterns were in universal cosmic perspectives; our perspectives surpass the underlying (current) anthropocentrism. Anthropocentrism is human perceptions of morality based in supernatural authority.

With anthropocentrism most of the current ideologies are centered in humanity's liberation yet they act as if they are unaware of the need for liberation of: Earth - Atmosphere – Ionosphere-Cosmos. Anthropocentrism causes humans to act from what I call "limited Scope Perspectives".

At the same time, our socialization; our social "Reflective Humanism" (which is human based perceptions of morality), enables us to liberate and to recognize beyond the anthropocentrism prevalent in many current doctrines globally, and can free us from their "financial feudalism".

DEFINITION. **Feudalism**, also called **feudal system** or **feudality**: a construct for designating the social, economic, and political conditions. "Financial feudalism" is a system of financial Aristocracy that is oppressive to the common man.

We advocate this: That which is the essence of Humans is fashioned in the image and the likeness of the INVISIBLE Giver of Breath, born before all creatures.

That means you are a part of that which created the celestial and terrestrial Universe, you are a part of the visible thing and the invisible thing. It means that the Giver of Breath is the pattern or beginning, and the end or completion of the Created Universe. "The One" is before everything and the Universe has in him, its consistency. Ahud, *ahud Is Yamassic for: one Love, one Respect, and one Justice. Reflective Humanism is an opposite to being anthropocentric.

Life is also part of the cycles that the cosmos makes, and with it, the essence of that which is conscious including humans resurges cyclically in kind. The revolutions are not events of nature giving man another chance, and they are not momentary, as man's small revenge on the tomb. That means that we are not talking about the religious concepts of death, the resurrection, or reincarnation that discussion is for religious leaders. We are speaking of scientifically measurable cosmic realities. We are speaking of tremendous comic Quantum Events.

Life emerges under the fire in each cosmic fight. During each cycle life lowers itself until the grave and from there life raises more and more in its recovery; until it integrates more and more into total harmony with the vibratory pulse of The Mother. Then it all begins again.

Indigenous human groups are sustained with the tradition that the "GREAT SPIRIT" is present from the beginning of creation and it impregnates everything. In our effort to overstand the Universe indigenous people appeal to the category of 'SPIRIT' for the overstanding of the contributions of the current cosmology".

REFLECTIVE HUMANISM SOCIALIZATION IN ACTION

When studying "Reflective Humanism Socialization" or the concepts of human based morality of indigenous people, consider that social problems like poverty, ignorance, and the destruction of the environment are problems for indigenous people across the world, but with different intensity and different tone of voice, and they demand urgent answers equally that all humans must be aware of.

Humans will come to solutions to the problems of Earth's Environment(s) such as the unchecked deforestation of Mother Earth when we all considered the differences between "indigenous people" and those that continue to ignore us; and when we begin fertile dialogues to establish a convergence of ideas that consider the connection that we the people (we the indigenous people) have with our environments.

> Master Popocatzin wrote: "I am happy to send them this, on the contrary I feel bad about it, but we (the Brother hood) are concerned with what happens and what might happen. My life has always been on the road of trying to change human mentality and trying to find better ways to achieve happiness, happiness not based on money, but in the creative work and the desire to be better.
>
> He said, I am happy to send them (you-all) this information of our activities globally, (HE IS SPEAKING OF THE COMMUNICATIONS WITH SCIENTIST AROUND THE WORLD. THEY HAVE DECIDED TO REENGAGE THE

INDIGENIOUS COMMUNITY FOR INPUT TOWARDS REMEDIES TO THE PENDING PLANETARY DISSASTERS) During recent years I have worked hard to study phenomena that occur on earth and they cause damage, my conclusion is that Mother Earth will continue to exist and that we disappear from the planet by our own will. We must make this happen.

*I've always said that Universe Creator speaks to me and sends me messages, so I was disqualified and even threatened by people because of my comment that the Universe Creator was willing to do away with man of the earth because of the evil man does, so I deluded them sometimes. I will tell you this **he sent his messengers thirteen in number of them seven men defend humans and six attack humans and are willing to give us death.***

*The first seven have made an extreme effort to give a chance to humans. **All messengers take human form and are here, have names and are acting**, those who defend the human right to continue on earth are losing the battle, currently the battle is lost to sight, **The Universe Creator has pointed out that five billion men will die** and of those who survive many will die because of them not knowing how to survive. All of this is because of mans' **ignorance and indifference to life close to nature, of those one billion to survive nearly all will die in the first year, and the*** *rest will have the opportunity to start a new life.* *This is a prediction that has a basis, but we still have time, we can still do something.*

If genetics put all their talents to the service of humanity. We can achieve a timely response is a matter of days or months, but we must act. I'm not biblical but it is the time to sow and keep natural seeds, not trans-genetic. Trans-genetic foods, this is action that will give ruin to life, we need to acquire fertile seeds and learn to survive. We must know what seeds, we must know how to use them, we must know where to go for best survival."

That was the conversation as it was presented to me on July 17th, 2010. The messages have described to us much of the sickness in our Mother, Earth, and her offspring, and it discusses with us **some cure or remedy.**

THE LEGEND OF THE EAGLE AND THE SNAKE
When analyzing the metaphoric symbolisms of the EAGLE AND THE SNAKE, we open a reflection of concepts of the development of indigenous human socialism in this land. The truth is that in the origins of the peoples of North America, Central America and South America, there is an important convergence.

"They left Chicomostoc (the place of seven caves) together in the search of the ideal places to settle. The people dispersed to seven towns, many of them in North America. The Mechica followed the itinerary until they arrived at a place (now call Mexico City) where the travelers found an eagle devouring a snake; also finding guidance to remain there in the center of the great lake that is dedicated to that symbol."

That it is the legend. If we analyze that symbolism in such a way that we deepen the construction of the reality in the study, and by carrying out a cosmology called Holism or Synergy, we can appreciate the interdependence of this natural convergence, and the importance of this to the indigenous people of North America.

This story demonstrates a philosophy of history of the cosmic-bicultural unitary specie, a single anthropology of all the indigenous people of this land now called America.

The symbolism of the eagle is present in the foundation of man's world and with him the opening capacity is of the look toward the future, and the transcendence toward the infinite. These are the utopias, dreams, yearnings, projections, and ideas that sustain us indigenous people like food, so that we never die and even when the dreams seem long made, or they seem that they may fail, we are always reborn with spontaneity, and in natural form. Among the Mechica YAMASSEE, the Eagle is a symbol of creativity, of light, of transparency, and of transcendence beyond the chaos.

The snake crawls and is contained, (she hides). The snake is symbolic of a weight in concrete history and in a concrete place; this is also the case with many of the projects in process today. It is symbolic of current social prevailing systems, daily life, habits, and customs that are the limitations that paralyze and impede dreams. Snake it is also a superiority symbol.

The social thought of native peoples is the fundamental principles of the Cosmos. The symbolic thing and the diabolical thing that represent the eagle and the snake respectively are two constituent and structuring principles of nature and of the cosmos, of social behaviors and of human nature; and that all share a dramatic coexistence. Both dimensions are present in the cosmic process of life; and in human beings; and they are necessary polarizations. They exist without dissociation or exclusion one from the other.

Eagle and Snake represent the unit and the differentiation, and they confer harmony to the dynamism of the Universe.

The dimension Eagle and Snake represents the energies that relate to the whole reality; to each other they are everything. Together they represent the opening, and it impels the evolution toward the future.

The dimension Snake represents a type of conservatism, that promotes progress inside the order, a stability that negates movement and the obstinacy of "I don't participate in the particles that reach a good position to receive the advantages of all the energy that is concentrated on the evolution of the Universe".

ENERGETIC COEXISTENCE

All the beings of the universe work from the same cosmic laws, the same cosmic particles, the same chemical compositions, and the same energies. In this sense the universe is Cosmos, Order, Harmony, Unit. But the Unit of the universe is not stationary or not one singular object; it is open to infinite probabilities, from the diversity of galaxies to stars, planets, moons, life and then sentient life.

In the Cosmos there is expansion and concentration, autonomy and interaction, order, and chaos. Each of these pairs coexist, when we divide the units, he, and she we introduce difference, and there is the diabolical and the symbolic, there is part, and there is everything.

In the Social Humanism of native people this coupling does not represent the duality that is supported in western culture, but rather they are tendencies of the Unique Unit of oneself movement, dimensions of oneself complex reality.

A co-creative system

We should consider that the Universe is an open, co-creative system, a directorial transport. The future is not derived lineally from its past neither of its present. The Universe moves in the field of probabilities. It is open to novelty; it could have the capacity of accidental/incidental emerges and of new synthesis. The genesis of this Galaxy is the Universe, we will discuss three characteristics that the Universe presents: Complexity, Relegation, and Interiority.

Complexity: consists of groups constituted by interrelated parts, its systems, and subsystems. Here we are speaking of the collective of galaxies, solar systems, planets, nebulas, and so on.

Relegation: rel-e-gate: (relegate) rel·e·gat·ed: rel·e·gat·ing: rel·e·gates ... to assign to a particular class or category; classify. Relegation is the act of assigning (someone or something) to a particular class or category. Relegation registers in a rich mesh of structures and beings each individually and collectively: each a part of **everything** that is ordered, all a part of "The All". Relegation finds its more brilliant materialization in the phenomenon of life that is self-conscious; sentient beings Interactive life represented in a double movement: 1. of adaptation to him; 2. of the means to her this is a natural component of "relegation". In the process of humans ending up complete beings we use these concepts to help us achieve strengthening of our relationships.

Interiority: Of, relating to, or located on the *inside*. Interiority is present in all the beings of the universe, but especially among who we call living beings that are endowed with a higher central nervous system, this is true in animals and is the same in the human being. In the Universe everything is interconnected. Human history is interconnected with the history of the universe, of Mother Earth, and of all life. Human history is not another history, but part of the only history, although Human history is a more complex and on a more conscious level.

It is the same thing with the social order, the social order is not a separated order, but rather it is integrated into a wider order. The true order is the history (order) of life, Mother Earth, and the Cosmos.

In other words, the history of the cosmos and social history is one. Such a position speaks directly to the separation from the anthropocentric paradigm, whose account is that the spirit is exclusive to the human species.

PART 3 ~

THE NEED TO CONSTRUCT WELL BALANCED ENVIRONMENTS

CONVERSATIONS
A dialogue delivered by Tlamatinime
Cuaupopocatzin (Lord of the Voice)

"We have been instructed to make well balanced environments. Concepts of Humanitarianism, Anthropocentrism even those of Atheism and others should cooperate in the construction of the new society.

To the religions, this corresponds to the function of recovering the integrative experience of the mystery of life and in consequence one of re-tying all things: cosmos and creation; spirit and body; conscious and unconscious; masculine and feminine; immanent and transcendent; nature and human beings; me and us.

We should not make the same conditions of subjection and oppression, of exploitation and of spoil, of alienation and of marginalization that are present in the political, financial, military and religious systems that make up the world temple, where they adore material wealth as "the god of LIFE" and they rob men; and they depredate Mother Earth.

Inside the Social Humanism of our native towns, we should analyze and act upon another challenge, that is the facilitating of new alliances, one with the different one, with the other one, to learn how to treat all as neighbors. We are not enemies, but allies; we Indigenous People are not an undivided people (undivided from the rest of the world community) and must not be seen as an occupational threat or an interference.

But we must be viewed with hopes, and act with cooperation with each other and with others. We should harbor spiritual thought that reties all humans together. We are to affirm that there is no longer man, neither woman, neither slave, neither liberal, neither conservative, neither I, Miss, Mr., or national, we all are one in the species human of earth; and this alliance should be reformed in the context of **planetary civilization**. There is no longer neither white nor black, neither native neither migrant, neither Westerner, neither Asian, neither believer neither non-believer. On this planet, we all have the same civic responsibilities.

Indigenous people in/on this land are all siblings; and are in the pursuit of the freedom of the Great Spirit Creative forces of the Galactic Universe, and we share *the same responsibility in the construction of a fairer world.*

These messages have been gathered starting from these words delivered through-out time, by many messengers of the Great Spirit of Creative Forces of the Galactic Universe. They are alignment positions that can represent the ideal objectives of the indigenous peoples that want to be a single people, human children of oneself mother that is Mother Earth, those that cohabit in harmony with the other beings of the Great Spirit, Giver of Breath Creative Forces of the Galactic Universe; our Father".

Another Conversation

He, my companion said, "The news from the Great Spirit Creative Forces of the Galactic Universe have been flowing like tree leaves in Autumn, human life runs serious risk of suffering the predictions of the indigenous sages and of current science. Humans have many concerns as to the cause of the destructive course that nature has taken at this time with storms of water and wind, hurricanes, typhoons, and tornados. These actions carry sweet water from the ocean to help to maintain the balance of life.

People are questioning without an answer as to Mother Earth's actions that are committed in the destruction process. I shared with him words of our beloved Master Mustafa, in his degree of the shaking what I had learned from Imam Isa:

Her Terrible Shaking

Master Mustafa English translation

Grand Chief Black Thunderbird Eagle

> When Mother Earth is shaken with her terrible shaking, And Mother Earth throws-up her burdens; and the people say, what is [wrong] with-her?" That day, she will tell her-news because your lord commands it for her. That day, the people will depart forward into groups/categories to see their-works (deeds). So, whoever does an atom's heaviness of good will see it, so whoever does an atom's heaviness of negativity will see it.

My companion said "The notices that I receive is sad and they make cry to my heart. You (Supreme Grand Chief Black-Hawk Thunderbird) have described it very well in your last test for the Chiefs of the Clans associated to the Nation Mechica and the MBC/INAAN".

The rebalance of Mother Earth is not going well. Our mother has decided to let go. She is beginning the terrible shaking as foretold by the sages and the ancients. In the pageant of life Mother Earth's continued existence is balanced in a specific marine salinity for life to flourish; this is also the case with the process of animal reproduction including in humans. Earth has lost its density like salt that has lost its savor, this it will continue with the breaking of her polar caps. Master Yashua said If salt has lost its savor how can it be useful but for dirt and sand to be walked upon. Unlike salt, In the case of Earth, could be we will not even be able to walk upon her for a time.

My companion said "Everything happens such and that I predicted in 1990 before the natives Chiefs when celebrating the Relief of the Mother Earth festival "TONANZIN CUATLICUY" where there was not one single representative of the native communities of North America; but you were the plants and the animals in extreme abundance on the platform where the NAVEL OF MOTHER EARTH is located.

In that celebration we made orderly predictions from the Creative forces of the Universe, and we point out the actions to continue to avoid the effect of the predictions that say, there would be a great cataclysm in 2012". **He said**, "My Boss Chief Black-Hawk " the cry in my eyes doesn't cease we are precipitating the end without reaching completion of our goals".

We needed money to act, or we needed the governments of the world to be devoted towards executing the rain tasks for inertia to take out the fresh water of the sea and to maintain the appropriate salinity that carried out actions of preservation of life in earth. We told them that they needed to stop clear cutting or the trees the deforestation that are detrimental to Earth's appropriate magnetic level.

Man thinks of the monopolizing of wealth and in the exploitation of the natural resources. The effect is visible; there are times that the imbalance makes us lose eight hours of one day, now there are times that we live 16 hours in a day instead of 24 hours. They forget about the negative that the abundance of physical wealth can have on the human mind. It is logical to rebalance the forces of the planet to avoid the man made, un-wanted physical vibrations and its' acceleration. The planet should turn at the same time rate that she makes comfortable changes in her

geographical positions to maintain her equilibrium (balance point). Earth preserves the level of the saline density with storms of long duration with great winds and large quantities of water in Hurricanes, typhoons, and tornados. In natural order this spreads water from the ocean to maintain the balance of the life on the planet.

Man does not do anything to help, on the contrary the extraction of gases, petroleum, minerals and by transporting these materials in large quantities from one place to another multiplies the problems; all of this contributes to Mother Earths' imbalance as we predicted in the year nineteen ninety.

With the changing effect of the rotational vibration of the planet an extraordinary mass of polar ice broke off. This contributed sweet water to the ocean causing a collapse in the salinity levels. The sudden batch of ice water caused an increase of the flow of fresh water need to oxygenate the water in the oceans that transport, nurture, and increase planetary life, That, caused a collapse in the balance of marine life in that area.

February of 2010 another polar mass came off in the area of the Antarctic Ocean, which are caused enormous risk. By the time that day passed the superficial life forms in the area had died due to ice burgs colliding one with the other. There was a great collapse of marine foods in the area where penguins and seals live. These life forms are being handicapped and prevented access to that area, and it is the inevitable end that we will witness.

Please remember, these conversations took place during the years 2008-2010. He said, "My heart cries because the native peoples should have been more convincing to the governments of the US Territory that they also attended to the solution. Many understood many actions of the project that you Grand Chief Black-Hawk Thunderbird announced, but the Great Spirit has indicated to me that it gives birth to acting because "everything is already irreversible" the Planet will suffer a great overturn where about 5 billion people may die"... I saw something else. My site was a little different, not much just a little. He then agreed. My companion went on to say..."This sickness is like a form of amnesia in the indigenous populations around the world, and America is no exception". I said, Indigenous people are here to do our part; to assist our Mother; and to aide our peoples in recovering from the amnesia.

"Our native people are a great human resource because they have survived all the wrongs of a mistaken society. Our people will suffer but they know how to survive where there is not anything". Indigenous Native American people have been performing active roles with projects designed to aide both Mother Earth and her children. We have been examining the sickness in Mother Earth from two perspectives,1. The mistreatment of the very planet herself; 2, regarding the mistreatment of the indigenous populations of America and their respective lands."

A LIVING ORGANISM

You must know that "Earth" is a living, breathing pulsating organism. Like all living organisms she has a specific balance. Like all living organisms she reproduces. All of the living organisms of Mother Earth are her offspring, including man". Man has been charged by the Giver of Breath and our Mother Earth with her upkeep and maintenance. This is truly a great honor. Man has allowed this honor to cause him to become very arrogant. Arrogance and cruel treatment to Mother Earth and her innocent children by some men, has caused much instability and sickness in Mother Earth and among her offspring. Man's Arrogance is a chief cause of the sickness". MBC/INAAN scientists, health officials and religious leaders are currently performing integral roles on projects working to address these two aspects of the mission to save our mother and ourselves. Our Mechica scientist in Mexico have worked on projects to assist at balancing the planets' orbit, her orbital speed, and her general stability in the galaxy with projects such as part of a "Rain for Inertia" project.

Rain for inertia: "Rain for inertia is part of a process for the reconstruction of Mother Earth's natural circuits restoring the interaction between the land and oceans; by the generation of rains.

Another of the objectives of this project is targeted at restoring the proper planetary weigh distribution by way of the rain runoff to designated locations. You should know that in seven occasions Mother Earth has suffered cataclysms that changed her face, these phenomena were associated to meteorites and to seven big floods, and the last is mentioned in the Bible. One of the men taught the science was Master Enoch. It is said among the

Image by Tlamatinime Cuaupopocatzin

brotherhood When this happened during his time, Master Enoch was warned by the Creative Forces of The Universe, and for many years he appears in Scotland where he built rain circles to control the waters of the seas and to reduce the effect of the flood which arrived from time to time, the Great Spirit taught him so that he could make the rain where it had been indicated.

The makers of the rain appeared in diverse parts of the planet. I was offered the information of rainmaking. I asked if that information could be passed on to one of my sons, and it wa given to my son Golden Eagle Thunderbird.

Many of you may be aware that man is the cause of much ecological disorder due to the clear cutting of the forests; improper waste disposal techniques and the removal and burning of fossil fuels. These are just some of the causes for the sickness in our mother".

In this day in time our Mechica scientists have developed a reactor that can be retrofitted to our homes and commercial facilities. The reactor converts trash and other household rubbish into reusable energy to provide an in-house power source to bring power to the facilities; while other MBC/INAAN health officials are teaching and preparing educational materials to guide in the wellbeing and balancing of the of the human mind and body. Our Shaman, Imams, Rabbis, and other ministers are educating daily, guiding us regarding spiritual and religious matters.

RECLAIMING THE LAND

MBC/INAAN educational institutions are providing the historical and cultural information of the historical presence of our people in this hemisphere; while our MBC/INAAN politicians and statesmen have achieved standing for people and are continuing to prepare standards for venues that demonstrate our re-emergence as a viable people in the international world.

These are some prescriptions towards the cure. The Great Spirit of the Universe Creator "Giver of Breath has directed us that we should unite and that all the **"native peoples come together"** and form a union and reclaim our position on this land. The Mund Bareefan Clan was not the only to receive this message.

From the indigenous people of Mexico and the Chiefs and Shaman:

This is the message that Tlamatinime Cuaupopocatzin (Lord of the Voice) brought to Grand Chief Black-Hawk Thunderbird, from the indigenous people of Mexico and the Chiefs and Shaman of the Natives Clans of America across the Rio Grande which flows from southwestern Colorado in the United States to the Gulf of Mexico.

September 19th and 20th, 2008... a big step was made on behalf of the indigenous people of America. My comments in this section are in light print. The Fall Equinox celebration lasted from the 19th thru the 21st of September. On the twentieth of September Master Tlamatinime Cuaupopocatzin (Lord of the voice) of the galactic brotherhood came to me Grand Chief Black Hawk Thunderbird. He greeted me asked me if I was Grand Chief Black-Hawk Thunderbird I answered "Yes" then he said, "I was sent to you".

I replied to him and why were you sent to me?

He explained "there has been a meeting of the chiefs and shaman of the indigenous people of America, and you were not there. "I said no we were not because we did not get the call, we had not received the invitation.

He said to me "I know" then he smiled and went on to say, "I was sent to you".

He spoke to me of the role that Mexico has to the magnetic grid of the planet. I was also told of the other electro-magnetic portal points.

It was revealed to us that our sibling in Mexico the MECHIKA truly acknowledge us as their brethren. He went on to explain that MUND BAREEFAN CLAN shall be their chosen seat of government and he expressed their interest for membership with the "Native American Association of Nations".

He spoke with me about the condition of mother earth and her people. He told me important facts about "global warming". He began to show me how they move water and how to bring water to the desert to re-green it, and how to aid in the rebalancing of the indigenous peoples; and he shared with me plans for the restoration of the natural environments of the planet. He demonstrated to me how to bring the hydrogen gas from water (H2O) to run our cars. He enlightened me on many other things so much to the point that I asked him if he wanted to address the people that very day.

His reply "Only if I can do it officially, only if I can perform the appropriate ritual ceremony. I must wear the official head-dress and perform the appropriate ritual ceremony to the Great Spirit of the Universe Creator. Can you wait until I return to my room and get prepared"?

At that point if not before it was clear to me and clear to all those listening, we were in the presence of an incredibly special person. He had come prepared to give us greetings and salutations from the indigenous people in America and with blessings from the Great Spirit of the Universe Creator. All I had to do was to accept. I agreed of course.

When he returned, he had a crown that was trimmed with liquid gold with pheasant feathers all around it. He put it on; the room was filled with energy the very moment he dawned the crown, everyone in the room could feel the energy then he began praying for the blessings, guidance, unity, and protection of the Great Spirit of the Universe

Tlamatinime Cuaupopocatzin

Creator, then repeating I pray for that, I pray for that, I pray for that, I pray for that. He began to speak raising his hands and voice turning toward the four cardinal points withTlamatinime Cuaupopocatzin" being the fifth cardinal point for this occasion connecting us all on that day and exclaiming at the direction of each cardinal point" I pray for that".

Here is the message as it was delivered. "A message from The Mechica Nation and from the more than 200 native clans and tribes that make up the 29,000 communities that exist **within the borders of Mexico**, still under the ancestral signs and customs, in the voice of Tlamatinime Cuaupopocatzin**(Lord of the voice)**, to the chiefs of the sister nations, clans and tribes that reside in the north American territory beyond Rio Grande; and to the Great Chief Black Hawk Thunderbird of the Yamassee Union upon the occasion of the ritual ceremony of the Fall Equinox celebrated on the 20th thru 21st of September 2008, in Lithonia Georgia.

Oh, venerable chiefs of the native peoples that are gathered here today, Great Honorable Chief of the Yamassee Union, Black Hawk Thunderbird, all of us being made brothers by a common past lived out by our ancestors". **Their descendants were among the first Blacks of pre-Columbian American origins who fell victim to kidnapping for the purpose of enslavement. Blacks of South America, the Caribbean and Central America were also attacked and enslaved.**

We have requested permission from the Great Spirit of the Universe Creator, we have invoked the powers, we have sent our word from the sacred mountaintops of our continent, and we have returned to the navel of Mother Earth, Tenochtitlan;

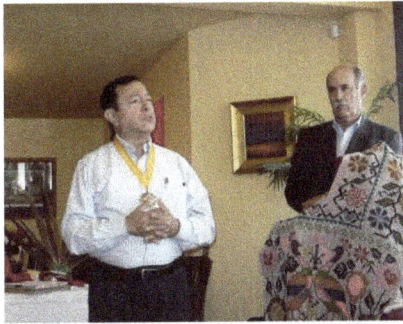

And from the heights of Grand Teocalli, who points to the center of balance of our Planet, from where is generated the magnetic energy that governs the world, from there we humbly elevate our plea to the five cardinal points, thereby making known our request that we could be here today and be part of this ritual ceremony. The message came back with a positive response the very day we raised our prayer. The great Spirit of the Universe Creator has ordered us to lay down a flowered carpet, **Xochipetla**"...

Gesura Red Silver-Fox Thunderbird is the guardian of the artifact for our Clan and for "NA-AN", The **N**ative **A**merican **A**ssociation of **N**ations. This artifact was hand woven for the very occasion by Clan Mother of the Mechica MBC/INAAN in Mexico.

..."so that we may go in together(that we create a union) to the twelfth heaven with the fruits of Mother

Earth, and thereby demonstrate our will for human integration and the will to perpetuate life on this planet, quality of life in harmony, respect, and solidarity amongst all living things. You all should know that the Great Spirit has told us that Mother Earth is extremely sick and is requiring that the native peoples on this continent and all the people under the Sun to come to her aid. She has told us that we cannot forget that she opened her bountiful womb and that from her sprang forth life itself; and that she permitted the necessary gifts so that all living beings could reproduce and populate her. Man, she has said, has contributed to the chaos and has broken the harmony and the unity that existed between space, time, nature, and the social order of the world, thereby placing in danger her vital capacity; Mother Earth is sick, and this sickness should be cured.

THE SUNS

The Mechica tradition predicts this: it is necessary to return to the rituals of Mother Earth and invoke the cosmic powers that they might come to our aid and put an end to this chaos. It tells us that it is the time for the sixth sun, the sun of unification and solidarity, a sun that will place us in vertical communication between Earth and sky, and IT will also horizontally bind the four corners of Mother Earth, united by the central point that is determined by each human.

The Great Spirit of Universe Creator tells us that earthly space reconstruction should be dominant and the rehabilitation of the environment and the powers of nature. We are also ordered to imitate the sacred order that reigns in the universe and there must be a cosmogonist reproduction wherein earthly space and the social order will be an exact mirror image of the cosmic order. It tells us that there is no more use of the fifth sun (the sun of movement), that essential widening sun where everything has found its obverse (Its' own face, or path (opposites).

It also tells us that now the sixth sun must reign, a sun of integration where we will all have a place, all the suns together – the sun of Mother Earth, the sun of fire, the sun of the wind, the sun of water".

MOTHER EARTH IS SICK AND THIS SICKNESS SHOULD BE CURED!!!

"The great Spirit of the Universe Creator has ordered us to lay down a flowered carpet so that we may go in together to the twelfth heaven with the fruits of Mother Earth, and thereby demonstrate our will for human integration and also the will to perpetuate life on this planet "Ammatum", quality of life in harmony, respect and solidarity amongst all living things. You all should know that the Great Spirit has told us that Mother Earth is extremely sick and is requiring that the native peoples on this continent and all the people under the Sun (to come together) and to come her aid"
~Lord of the Voice

PART 4 ~

THE POLITICS OF CURING MOTHER EARTH

Did you know that if you are Native American and you **choose** to pass as an African American, your leaders must re-establish your right to vote in America every given number of years? That means that you are not even fully accepted citizens of your citizens of your **chosen** Government.

I will share with you one condition that African Americans must deal with that a Guale Yamassee Native American does not have to face, and that is the right to vote. The African Americans right to vote in America is decided by people other than African Americans. Why? African Americans are conditional US citizens and have already chosen or made their choice or determination as to their nationality or the right to self-governance, which means African Americans have very little if anything at all to say in most of the governmental matters that concern Black African Americans as a people. That is real sickness.

All Guale Yamassee Native Americans who **chooses** to vote in America maintain the right to vote in America perpetually. Here is remedy, and a true and sure prescription for cure. Guale Yamassee Native Americans possess full Indigenous Rights to self-determination, "Autonomy" by virtue of:

- The MBC/INAAN Guale Yamassee Native American Constitution
- The "Constitution of the United States of America and the "Bill of Rights"
- MBC/INAAN Guale Yamassee Native Americans Code Annotated
- The Mund Bareefan Constructive Agreement with the United States 2/11/2004
- The Treaty of Camp Holmes 1835, to which we are an associated nation
- The internationally ratified "Declaration of the Rights of Indigenous Peoples"

- Over two hundred years of American case law both prior to and after the undeclared federal, corporate United States government bankruptcies of 1930-1938.

"We have also given our sacred oath to protect and defend the Living Constitution of The Guale Yamassee Native Americans (MBC/INAAN); and to honor the Constitution of United States of America against all enemies, both foreign and domestic".

The current world political condition is just another part of the **sickness,** especially if you know that you are Native American and you are passing as African American or if you know that you are African American and you are passing as Native American. Now all the American governments, and their commercial ways have saturated this land with large communities and big buildings disturbing the balance of nature and the flow of the natural energies of our environments and our intellect.

When the Europeans came to our shores, the Guale Yamassee people were people of the woods, we built our communities small and in tune with the rest of the natural environment. In this way we maintained balance with the nature within our environment.

Guale Yamassee Life and habitat had different kinds of living structures, many were mound shaped many were rectangular, made of wood pine straw, mud, and clay. These structures were as large as 50 to 100 feet in diameter. Some buildings were for communal functions and social gatherings, some were living space. There were structures for commercial usages like trading, to conduct clan/tribal business; and some were Massagiyd and the Christian Missions.

Massagiyd is a plural form of the word masjiyd. A Masjiyd is a place of worship for Muslims. Pre-Columbian America was well acquainted with Islam. As I said many structures were earthen mound temples where Chiefs and Clan Mothers met to council and to set clan/tribal business.

There were as many as 80 to 120 people to a village; many villages became tribes, as tribes expanded, they made up larger clans, chiefdoms on up to the confederation type alliances.

The Europeans have built large buildings in large communities and have disturbed the balance of the nature and the electromagnetic flow of our natural energy grid. Accept it or not this practice has caused much damage to us, plant life and our land; thereby it has caused damage to our Mother Earth.

A most effective remedy or cure to this part of the sickness... is the reestablishing of our Indigenous Native American ways, ceremonial rites, common law rights and Guale Yamassee civil and statutory rights and responsibilities to self-determination.

Indigenous peoples should not seek civil rights as these are determined by the controlling government that grants them.

As indigenous peoples were also enslaved by the Europeans, our stories are intertwined, and INAAN people continue to **actively** support our African American sisters and brothers in the struggles with civil rights. We/I have never registered as an African

American. When I was young my mother mentioned to us (her children) on more than one occasion that we are not African American. My mother said we have "Indian" blood in us, so in the sixties when most other Negros (blacks) became African American we/i did not follow. We in my mothers' family were speared that part of the sickness. At that time, we in my mothers' family just as in many other families, we just considered ourselves as whom we are, Black Native Americans. As we were in the black community our family would join in very actively in the struggle with African American for civil rights.

What we have found out through all those years is that where there is no jurisdiction, there is no remedy because what you know as civil rights are legislated by others. **This is another part of the sickness we are speaking of**.

To reiterate, because this is an important point, did you know that if you are Native American or African American, your leaders must re-establish your right to vote in America every given number of years?

That means that you are not even fully accepted citizens of your **chosen** Government.

I will share with you one condition that both African Americans and Indigenous Native American must face, and that is the right to vote. The African Americans and Indigenous Native American right to vote in America is decided by people other than African Americans and Indigenous Native American. Why? African Americans and Indigenous Native American are conditional US citizens and have already chosen or made their choice or determination as to their nationality or the right to self- governance, which means African Americans and Indigenous Native American have little if anything at all to say as self-determined peoples in most of the governmental matters that concern Black African Americans and Indigenous Native American in America. That is real sickness.

A most effective remedy or cure to this part of the sickness... is the reestablishing of our Indigenous Native American ways, ceremonial rites, common law rights and Guale-Yamassee civil and statutory rights and responsibilities to self-determination. And that is what we Mund Bareefan Embassy Clan/Indigenous Native American Association of Nations did and do.

INDIGENOUS SELF-DETERMINATION

ᕓᐅᕙᐣᕈᕠᕈᕋᐢᕋᕐᕐᕐᕟ ᐪᕐᕟᕓᕤ ᕙᕟ "ᕁᕐᕄᕁᕄ ᕄᕟᕤᕄᕐᕈ ᕉᕐᕊᕃ ᕌᕐᕊᕤᕄᕐ"

ᕙᕁᕓᕁ ᕐᕌᕔ ᕁᕐᕟᕤᕄ ᕄᕟᕊᕤᕈᕁ; ᕁᕐᕠᕓᕃ ᕄᕟᕊᕤᕈᕁ
ᕠᕐᕐᕃᕤᕋ ᕃᕟᕊᕤᕄᕁ ᕠᕐᕋᕀ ᕊᕐᕃᕤᕋ ᕠᕐᕈᕤᕠᕁᕓᕁᕁ ᕊᕈ
ᕙᕟ ᕄᕓᕊᕤᕁ. ᕙᕁᕓᕁ ᕐᕌᕔ ᕐᕋᕀᕐᕄᕐᕋᕁ ᕍᕟᕟ ᕙᕟ
ᕐᕌᕈᕀ, ᕙᕟ ᕄᕧᕤᕀ, ᕙᕟ ᕠᕐᕁᕤᕤ, ᕙᕟ ᕀᕓᕤᕤ, ᕙᕟ
ᕁᕓᕤᕟ, ᕁᕟ ᕙᕟ ᕐᕀᕃ. ᕙᕁᕓᕁ ᕠᕐᕟᕋᕟᕐ ᕁᕓᕟᕁᕓᕃ
ᕠᕐᕀ-ᕟᕧ ᕙᕟ ᕃᕐᕁᕁᕈᕀ ᕊᕧᕟ ᕁᕐᕃᕟᕁ ᕃᕐᕁᕓᕟ ᕙᕟ
ᕁᕐᕁᕠᕈᕀᕊᕠ ᕧᕌ. ᕠᕐᕀ-ᕟᕧ ᕙᕟ ᕃᕐᕁᕁᕈᕀ ᕊᕧᕟ ᕁᕐᕃᕟᕁᕁ
ᕙᕁᕓᕁ ᕠᕐᕊᕤᕀᕤ, ᕁᕐᕁᕄᕐᕟ ᕄᕌᕁᕐᕀᕁᕐᕁᕧ ᕠᕐᕀ ᕙᕟ
ᕁᕓᕄᕧ ᕊᕧᕟ ᕁᕟ ᕟᕧ ᕠᕐᕀᕟ ᕠᕓᕁᕠᕓᕄ. ᕁᕟᕠᕓᕀ-
ᕄᕟ ᕀᕃᕃᕟᕟ ᕁᕌᕁ ᕙᕟ ᕁᕓᕀᕟ ᕁᕟ ᕐᕀᕃ ᕊᕧᕟ
"ᕐᕁᕁᕁᕟᕁᕁᕃᕁᕁ" ᕈᕄᕁᕁᕋᕁᕁᕁ-ᕁᕐᕟ. ᕁᕟᕠᕓᕀ-ᕄᕟ
ᕠᕐᕟᕓᕁ ᕀᕐᕀᕐᕠᕟ ᕁᕄᕁᕟᕁ ᕠᕐᕁᕤᕀ, ᕀᕐᕐᕃᕤᕟ ᕁᕌᕁ
ᕙᕟ ᕀᕄᕀᕄᕐᕟᕟᕁ ᕊᕧᕟ ᕠᕐᕄᕤᕁᕀ ᕀᕐᕁᕤᕀᕤᕀ ᕃᕓᕠ
ᕠᕐᕟᕓᕁ ᕠᕐᕐᕃᕤᕀ ᕃᕐᕊᕤᕁᕁ ᕁᕌᕁ ᕠᕐᕁᕀ ᕐᕀᕃ.
ᕀᕄᕀᕄᕐᕟᕁ-ᕄᕟ ᕁᕄᕃᕤᕃ, ᕁᕟ ᕐᕁᕀᕄᕠᕁ-ᕄᕟ ᕠᕐᕠᕤᕄ

CᎡ᠌᠌ᏌᏯᏌ Ꮧ᠊ᏌᏀᏬ ᏗᏌᏌ᠌ᎧᏌᎤ ᏊᏌᏢᏌᏌᏟ ᏌᏌᏕᏌᏭᏌᏬᎤ ᏌᏟᏌᏌ
ᏔᏌᏌᏌ ᏌᏋᎧ ᏔᏌᏬᏬᎬ ᏗᏌᎧᏌᏯ ᏌᎤᏕᏬᎤᏤ᠊Ꮼ. ᏬᏠᏬᏠ
ᏌᏘᏌ ᏦᏌᎧᏌᏯᏌ "ᏟᏌᏌᎧᏌᏨ ᏗᏌᏬᏌᏌ ᎢᏌᏕᏌ
ᏘᏌᏌᏬᏌ" ᏬᏠᏬᏠ ᏌᏘᏌ ᏊᏌᏔᏌᏟᏌᏘᏬ.

~Recitation Life "The Sothern Cult"

Translation: "We are pure energy; a single thought manifesting with a double movement in the cosmos. We are kin to the ethers, the fire, the air, wind, the water, and Mother Earth. We are conceived within the cycles of time within this Universe. With the turn of time we manifest, brought through by the nature of and for this planet. Our essence has grown from the water and soil of "Earth" our Mother. Our essence is shared among many, stemming from the branches of a great tree that sprang forth from this land. Our branches extend, and our foliage continues to spread like a canopy across this Land now called America. We are called "The "Southern Cult". We are "Indigenous"...

I have prepared this work to speak with you about "Indigenous People" v. "Sovereignty".

Firstly, the founding Clan/family of the Yamassee Union of the nineties, is the La Tama Clan **(Tama Re Clan)** of Chief Black Thunderbird Eagle," this clan is of "House Thunderbird".

The first convention of the Yamassee Union took place on the land called Wahani and Tama Re, which was in Eatonton Georgia. We were chartered in 1995, as part of "The Union".

We are the Mund Bareefan Clan also of "House Thunderbird". Mund Bareefan Clan is a "legally authenticated" Guale/Yamassee Native American clan. In accord with MBC Constitution and international laws as related to indigenous peoples, Mund Bareefan Clan of "Royal Thunderbird" made; and along with other associated tribes and clans formed the Indigenous Native American Association of Nations.

The Authenticated Clan (of March 2003) and Executive Branch of our Association of Nations is the Mund Bareefan Clan of Maku Black-Hawk Hommie Thunderbird. Aka Derrick Hommie Sanders. The two principal families of these clans together that is the

"Mund Bareefan Clan" and the "La Tama Clan" together are "House Thunderbird" also called "Royal Thunderbird".

Our Association is established, Authenticated, and acknowledged Federally and in the sevel States, of the United States, "In fact".

> "**Our heroes** are not individuals who are raised up with a history which remained written in the past; the heroes in our tradition are those who gave their lives in an effort to reach the objectives of history written as the future by the ancients, **building for generations that would follow the steps; and they were dedicated to that history that was forthcoming, the history of the clans and the tribes, dedicated to the future that was already written.** Future and history were united with the life to come and with the dead past which was already gone".
>
> Cuaupopocatzin

Our position is that Indigenous peoples should live as autonomous, self-determined, self-governing peoples, not as individual sovereigns".

Q. Is it mandatory for indigenous and Aboriginal people to expatriate or surrender their US citizenship?

A. MBC-INAAN nationals are advised not to expatriate. That would not be in the best interests of the people. As Indigenous people in the United State, we inherently have what many people would love to have, dual citizenship. Why give it away?

About the Sovereignty movement: MBC-INAAN people do not seek acknowledgement of status thorough the current Sovereignty Movement techniques.

Some have construed our efforts as part of the Sovereignty movement, it is not. When you fight the Sovereignty battle, you fight a battle that can only be won by the officials that are charged by the specific government that made its codices, its manuals, rules and regulations; its practices and procedures for its own internal security against its adversaries; which set the protocols for **its internal implementation, and that's the way it works.**

With the sovereignty movement we are expected to challenge well established legal standards which have been being perfected for hundreds of years with the proficiency of an attorney in a courtroom. We have not experienced it working for an indigenous nation once. We have seen progress for some individuals but only for the short term, then it always has come back on the user(s) as unsuccessful and can cause emotional, legal and financial injury.

Many indigenous people today are attempting to communicate their presence to the independent governments that control their ancestral lands or lands that they legally occupy, and to other governments around the world. These international type communications can reach legal standing **if you are indigenous, and you have established legal standing by exercising self-determination (Autonomy)** with an Acknowledged and or Recognized Indigenous Agency with standing, and then only if one knows how to use them. Still, be prepared to fight for your rights, but this time with the best tools, indigenous rights, not civil rights, not sovereignty.

Q. Should we band together and form a tribe and then make legal demand for self-determination as indigenous people?

A. You're on the right tract, but there's a little more involved. You must be able to demonstrate that you are an indigenous people. The best way to do this is by checking with your elder family members. You should check there first.

You must be able to show that your tribe/clan is a member of an authentic indigenous people in time, and/or that you have been accepted and registered into a standing indigenous tribe/clan. If you are not authentic, you could be doing fraud. Your tribe/clan must be part of an authentic Acknowledged or Recognized Indigenous entity, with an established system of laws.

Q. Can we make-up a new tribe/clan and claim these rights?

A. We would not recommend that. There are quite a number of bonified indigenous agencies. Figure out which one you belong to or would like to belong to and inquire.

In this day in time Indigenous Peoples consider our position in the world as autonomous peoples by ourselves first, then to the independent governments that occupy our ancestral lands or lands we lawfully occupy.

The "I am" sovereignty techniques, is something quite different. There is no unity in the processes. You are alone on an island or left alone, to navigate through numerous court battles.

Or you may still be under the misconception that The Universal Declaration of Human Rights, or The Constitution of/for the United States of America at the time of the writings, were written with "Indigenous Peoples," "African Americans", or other "Ab-Original Peoples" in mind, they were not. Nor did The Universal Declaration "see" in the legal sense, our Governments, Clans, our Tribes, alliances and associations.

Indigenous and Ab-Original people were not seen as autonomous, nor parties to their Universal Declaration. Those governments only saw and continue to see Indigenous and Ab-Original people as under their jurisdictions.

House Thunderbird, with many other families, began our quest as an autonomous people in the 70s', with an ecumenical religious community. We just did not perceive how progressive it was.

This religious community was made of Muslims, then others joined in. there were Hebrews, Christians, Nuwaubians, Moors, Egyptologist, and others; all Indigenous Americans, all declaring their indigenous roots, most from clans of the Muscogee, and Algonquin stock, all of indigenous blood of North America.

We did not realize in the beginning that the indigenous bloodlines would be the force that would maintain our unity.

Twenty plus years later, at Mund Bareefan we found ourselves reading tools like "Breaking the Code" which introduced the "Redemption Movement/processes". We read and for a short period of time, a very short time, we used the "Breaking the Code" publications. This was introduced through the "Sovereignty Movement". We learned that is not for MBC-INAAN.

Think about it, you walk into a court room and present your documentation to the Judge; documentation which states that the court room that you have just entered, and the Sitting Judge is without jurisdiction over you. The judge now knows that you do not know law. Every sitting judge has jurisdiction.

First, the judge needs to determine if you are a foreigner. Well guess what, legally speaking you are not a foreigner, but you already knew that. You are a US American citizen. Actually, this could be a rather good thing. We will talk about that sometime.

Any way... next, the case may be about international commerce, or non-negotiable paper, or taxes or your sovereign status; and your "Brief in Support" or "Memorandum of Understanding", Act of State, or Public Notice, is loaded with US CODE, FRCP, Uniform Commercial Code (UCC), Rules of evidence. Sometimes the Oath of the KLU KLUK KLAN is used in these fillings.

You may have filed some form from a United States agency's Human Resources (HR) Department that surveys their employees, or some other United States protocols which cannot relate to you as an employee nor to being sovereign, nor to the court in relation to you other than as a US citizen. Why? Because you were born in the United States.

Remember, you presented documents to the court that outlines that you are foreign to their jurisdiction. You told them you are your own jurisdiction; or that the "STRAW MAN" in question is under your jurisdiction.

As a foreigner, you, the real live flesh and blood human which Indigenous people are, we all are, have no standing to bring "this type" case before "their court". You were born in the United States, and as the US American court sees you, you can be detained, fined, or incarcerated and sentenced to do time.

These practices are used with the "Sovereignty Movement". These tactics were developed by factions of the "Patriate Movement".

We never use this term sovereignty anymore. You will **not** find this term sovereignty in the UN Universal Declaration of the Rights of Indigenous Peoples. This term is not proper for Indigenous and Ab-original Peoples. We no-longer use the term in our Constitutions nor in our MBC-INAAN Code Annotated.

Sovereignty type law is not the type of law the INAAN is using. It is too combative, and it is an adversary to "Reflective Human Socialization". To INAAN people, these tactics are about the individual, the "I am" not about "We" the people.

If you are indigenous and you take yourself there, and your brief is loaded with the above authorities as your principal support, do you realize that you are using their shields or someone else's as your protection? Things that make you go, Hmmm!!!

First, as an indigenous individual/person you should not have reason to be in their court. Why? Because indigenous and Ab-Original people are law abiding. We respect the law, "ours" and "theirs". That's another lesson.

Understand something about the UCC

§ 1-103. Construction of Uniform Commercial Code to Promote its Purposes and Policies: Applicability of Supplemental Principles of Law.

(a) The Uniform Commercial Code must be liberally construed and applied to promote its underlying purposes and policies, which are: (1) to simplify, clarify, and modernize the law governing commercial transactions; (2) to permit the continued expansion of commercial practices through custom, usage, and agreement of the parties; and (3) to make uniform the law among the various jurisdictions.

(b) Unless displaced by the particular provisions of the Uniform Commercial Code, the principles of law and equity, including the law merchant and the law relative to capacity to contract, principal and agent, estoppel, fraud, misrepresentation, duress, coercion, mistake, bankruptcy, and other validating or invalidating cause supplement its provisions".

If you use the UCC as the/a principal biases for your notifications of status, remember, one needs to know that you need the **"permission of the Permanent Editorial Board for the Uniform Commercial Code for the limited purposes of study, teaching, and academic research"**.

If you are an indigenous people in the United States and are seeking to express yourselves, you must do it together, not as individual sovereigns whatever that really means. If you are in the United States, do not be tricked by those who cannot produce legitimately approved certification "of their own" with endorsement from the people, then with/from an established "Acknowledged" and or Recognized Indigenous Governmental Agency.

Q. *Can you tell me your internationally recognized legal national status in the United States and around the world?*

A. *Most people in the United States melanin dominant or not, are legally documented US citizens. That's not a bad thing, it's simply the reality. As such, you don't have an internationally recognized nationality* **as** *members of an autonomous, indigenous, self-determined people.*

There are several "Acknowledged" and or Recognized Indigenous Governmental Agencies. Do your due diligence.

LAWS OF NATIONALITY

Indigenous people are unaware of the laws of nationality. When we are children, we take on the nationality our parents have chosen. What we ignore is that when we are grown, we have the right, the obligation to declare who we are. If you don't, you continue to carry the nationality designation assigned at birth.

"Indigenous people" in the United States, have had our autonomy, nationality and ethnicity chosen and assigned by colonizing governments for hundreds of years. This reality has caused some to forget original birthright, original nationality to this land, and thus, many have lost memory of their birthright nationality and ethnicity as Indigenous Native Americans.

We use ethnic and religious titles like Negro, Black American, Chicano, Latino American, Moorish American, Nuwaubian, African American, Muslim, Ansar, Christian, and there are others. These are good honorable things to be. Some of these titles we consider national/international designations as autonomous, but they are not.

None of the above titles gives you international recognition as Autonomous Indigenous Peoples in the United States. Concerning the people of the MBC-INAAN as Individuals, we continue in our chosen faiths.

Jointly we exist as indigenous peoples we are". We lay claim, that we are indigenous peoples with personal, historical, State, and US Federal Acknowledgement of our birth rights as the indigenous the peoples we are. Remember this:

> *"These international type communications can reach legal **standing if you are indigenous and have established legal standing by exercising self-determination (Autonomy)** with an "Acknowledged" and or*

Recognized Indigenous Agency with standing"... quoted from above in this presentation. The following is MBC-INAAN Law, and international law.

1. INDIGENOUS NATIVE AMERICAN ASSOCIATION OF NATIONS CONSTITUTION "Bill of Rights", Article 5

   Every indigenous individual has the right to a nationality

2. UN DECLARATION OF THE RIGHTS OF INDIGENOUS PEOPLE, Article 6

   Every indigenous individual has the right to a nationality

3. UN UNIVERSAL DECLARATION OF HUMAN RIGHTS, Article 15

(a) Everyone has the right to a nationality

(b) No one shall be arbitrarily deprived of his nationality nor denied the right to change his nationality

4. INDIGENOUS AND TRIBAL PEOPLES PRACTICE: ILO CONVENTION NO. 169 ...identity, Article 6

Every indigenous individual has the right to a nationality

Maybe you're Indigenous, or maybe you're African, or maybe you are African American, or you may be a combination of all of the above. Considering the right to self-determination, it's your right, your obligation to choose. Be sure that you do your due diligence.

*Note: In the United States and internationally we are the Mund Bareefan Embassy Clan of House Thunderbird, a self- determined, Authentic, Acknowledged Indigenous family/clan. We are Guale also correctly called Yamassee Indigenous Native Americans, with the legal acknowledgement of and the legal capacity of self-determination, and self-governance.

In English that is MT. A'rafat Clan/tribe. In our language "Gabelu" is the word for tribe and clan, and sometimes used for family.

The meaning of our tribal name "Mund Bareefan" is, **"The place where the people know who they are"**. Our chosen tribal designation is "Guale" and "Guale-Yamassee".

LINEAGE TO THE LAND

My immediate family has lived and many if not most remain in and around Yamassee historical lands in Allendale, Barnwell, Beaufort, and Hampton counties in the South Carolina lowlands before the Europeans arrived there, and until this day continuously.

Our family and other Guale and Yamassee people are descendants of the Anu-Twa people of Ghana West Africa. They who **migrated** to North America thousands of years ago. Then came the Europeans. The Anu-Twa people are called the "Sonqua People" the in South Africa.

The name of what is now Costal Georgia was named Walie by the Europeans pronounced Guale in our languages.

Costal Georgia was originally named Guale for the Indigenous Chiefdom there before it was called Georgia; and is the home of the associated chiefdom of La Tama, home of the Yamassee. The La Tama Chiefdom was also called Altamaha, and was located within Georgia, or in "Guale" along the Altamaha River.

First encounters between our peoples and the Europeans in North America were in South Carolina, Georgia, and Florida. Some of these encounters would take place on the Barrier Islands of Guale (**Georgia)**, Orista (**South Carolina)**, and La Florida (**Florida)**. Some names of the Islands were: Zapala, Asao, Ospo, Tacatacuru and Daufuskie Island.

In Georgia there were also towns on the mainland like Altamaha, Chiefdom of the Yamassee La Tama tribe, and Tolomato and Talaxe. Tamucua, was to the south in Florida, which would part of La Florida as named by the Spanish. South Carolina was named "Orista" by the Spanish. Daufuskie Island is now a part of Beaufort South Carolina. All of this and more was Guale and Yamassee territory. Yamassee people are recorded in South Carolina History to have lived on Daufuskie, nine (9) thousand Years before the Europeans arrived on the Island.

The Fascinating History Behind South Carolina's Timeless Daufuskie Island by Zach Bjur Hilton Head, SC May 9, 2016:

> ... There have been people living on Daufuskie from thousands of years ago till modern day, meaning there are artifacts from nearly every time period imaginable.

> Roughly 9,000 years ago, the island was home to Native American tribes like the Yemassee. They thrived in the area. The first incursion by Europeans occurred in 1521 when Spain claimed the coast spanning from St. Augustine to Charleston (Charles Towne at the time).

THE MBC-INAAN CONSTITUTION & FAQ

The following is for your private use: You may teach from it. You may use it as supportive educational material. Do not distribute with others.

The answers to the following questions are from the perspectives of the laws of the MC/INAAN; and are written to assist the education of the nationals of the MBC-INAAN.

Caveat: The unauthorized use of the MBC-INAAN Constitution, law(s), code(s), statute(s), etc. by parties in any lawful tribunal(s) for purposes of litigation, notice, or declaration, may be prosecuted. Parties should consult an MBC-INAAN official representative and/or retain proper official lawful representation.

Violators will be prosecuted under penalty of MBC-INAAN law for the unauthorized use of the MBC-INAAN Constitution, law(s), code(s), statute(s), etc. Please consult with the Guale-Yamassee Accredited Registry (GAR).

1. **What exactly is the role of an MBC-INAAN clan mother?**

   (a) An MBC-INAAN clan mother is one of the mothers or elder females of an MBC-INAAN clan.

   (b) The Clan Mothers are the group of mothers and elder females of a clan and have the capacity to be and should be involved in many decision-making process in a clan, as well as in the central government.

   (c) It is usually the clan Mothers that organize most official cultural activities of the clan.

Your local clan is encouraged to adopt this format for your local policies. Women may ascend to the rank of Clan Mother, Chief or any other administrative position in our Association of Nations.

MBC-INAAN Constitution Article 18 Section 13

   If Any Proposal Shall Not Be Returned
   by The Supreme Grand Chief Within Six
   to Eight Weeks, The Council May Call

the Principal chief **or the Council of Clan Mothers for consultation To Find Out the Status.**

MBC-INAAN Constitution Article 19 Section 1

Legislative Branch: Principal Chief Prime Minister, the High Governing Council, **and the Council of Clan Mothers.**

MBC-INAAN Constitution Article 19 Section 3.

The Privy-Council of Clan Mothers: shall function as "Executive Special Council" to the Gesura and **shall have the privilege of oversight in ALL government decisions**; The Privy-Council of Clan Mothers with the consent of the SGM, **shall have the capacity with a two thirds majority of the Governing High Council, to override the veto of the Principal Chief–Prime Minister or the SGC".**

MBC-INAAN CODE ANNOTATEDTITLE 21 § 1–114. Maintenance of minutes, bills, laws and resolutions

Original copies of laws and Tribal Resolutions: Three (3) original copies of all laws and resolutions shall be prepared by the Governing High Council Secretary. One (1) original copy shall be distributed to the Office of the Principal Chief Prime Minister, **one (1) original copy shall be distributed to the Council of Clan Mothers, and one (1) original copy shall be retained by the Governing High Council.**

These are sections from the laws of the MBC-INAAN that demonstrate the importance of the MBC-INAAN Clan Mothers. The Clan Mothers are sighted 14 times in our laws and clearly hold a very prominent position.

2. Should every Clan have clan mothers?

Yes.

3. What is the difference between local clan mothers and the "National Forum of Clan Mothers" (NFC)?

The National and Privy Council(s) of Clan Mothers:

MBC-INAAN Constitution Article 19 Section 3. B.

(a) The Gesura shall choose her own personal Privy-council of Clan Mothers.

(b) Each tribe/clan may have two representatives to the Nation council of Clan Mothers. The National Council of Clan Mothers is chosen from each clan to the National Council of Clan Mothers.

4. Who can become a clan mother?

The mothers and elder women of the clan are the clan mothers.

(a) Is there an age requirement? That shall be the choice of each clan.

(b) Is there a difference between elder women of a clan and Clan others? Yes, appointment.

5. What are the roles of the various Chiefs?

Pulled from the Constitution "Article 19 powers"

Supreme Grand Chief (SGC): Executive Power is granted by this constitution to the Supreme Grand Chief of said clan, that is the Mund Bareefan Guale-Yamassee Clan, of "House Thunderbird

Principal Chief Prime Minister: Shall be the Executive Director of the MBC/Indigenous Naïve American Association of Nations government

Have veto power which can be overturned by the SGC or two third majority vote by the Governing High Council and the council of Clan Mothers

Shall Carry the responsibility to authorize business under the seal of the MBC-INAAN which shall not the equal in authority the seal of the SGC; but shall be sufficient for Association business not needing the seal of the SGC.

The office of the Principal Chief shall not exercise undue authority over The Governing High Council".

Section 3 BRANCHES OF GOVERNMENT and SEPARATION OF POWERS

The sitting chiefs of the MBC-INAAN Assembly The location for Sessions:

Principal Chief Prime Minister: The sitting chiefs of the MBC-INAAN assembly Will Choose the incoming Principal Chief Prime Minister of the MBC-INAAN and Secondary Chiefs of the MBC-INAAN. The Supreme Grand Chief and Council of Clan Mothers will consent or not. If the Council of Clan Mothers and or the SGC rejects the candidates, the process must begin again. The Person(s) Having the unanimous agreement of the SGC, Council of Clan Mothers and the Governing High Council Shall Be the Principal Chief (PM), and Secondary Chief of THE INAAN.

6. **What should a national do if they have a problem with a Chief's official behavior?**

This should be reported to the tribal Chief and the tribal clan mothers.

7. **What is the role of Nationals?**

To obey the laws and to be of service and support to the Nation.

8. **Are there national elections for the entire Association or clans?**

Yes.

MBC-INAAN Constitution Article 18 Section 2

> The Government of The Mund Bareefan Clan-Indigenous NATIVE AMERICAN ASSOCIATION OF NATIONS Is A Republic; and chooses Officials with A Democratic Form of Governing. **All Seats of The Chiefs, And All other Council Seats of The Association Government Shall Be Filled by Election by The People**; and Approved by The A'zum Akbur Maku (Supreme Grand Chief). The Attorney

General Shall Be appointed by the Supreme Grand Chief).

Article 18 Section 8

The time, place, and manner of holding elections for officials and representatives, shall be approved in each Clan/Tribe by a High Council there/of.

TITLE 19, § 1–102 ELECTIONS

§ 1–102. General elections

On the Saturday immediately following the first Saturday of November, and every four (4) years thereafter, a general election shall be held, at which time the Principal Chief Prime Minister and the Second Chief of the MBC-INAAN shall be elected. On the Saturday immediately following the first Friday of November, and every two (2) years thereafter, the Governing High Council representatives shall be elected.

9. What happens to Clans or Nationals that do not participate in their financial obligations?

This could lead to legal action, fines and or dis-fellowship.

The Power to Dis-fellowship. Part 5, Article 18

§ Section 4: The Power to Dis-fellowship:

> If Any Member of a Clan/Tribe Is Found in Abuse of The Laws Set and Agreed Upon by That Governing Body, They Will Be Dis-fellowshipped. Governing High Council Can Reinstate A Member Depending on The Circumstances and By Vote of The Body That Dis-fellowshipped Her\Him.

10. Does the national government or Clans have a spiritual leader or Shaman?

The spiritual leader of a tribe is the in the domain of the clan. The government has no jurisdiction in spiritual matters unless they are deemed constitutionally unlawful or invasive of privacy of others   in   the   community.

The official Shaman for the Mund Bareefan Clan proper is Shaman Climbing Tall Oak, of House Thunderbird

11. Is there a vital statistics Branch or office within the national government?

Yes.

MBC-INAAN Code Annotated:

Title 2 NATIONALITY/CENSUS, § 1–101. Title and codification:

> This Law of the MBC-INAAN shall be known and may be cited as the MBC-INAAN nationalization/membership Code and shall be codified in Title 2, of the MBC-INAAN CA.

12. How do I get a birth certificates or IDs for my clan? Or tribal members?

Contact the INARS office.

(a) What is the turnaround time? Two (2) weeks

(b) Is emergency/next day service available? If so, how much? Not currently.

13. How may I get an official name change?

This is an administrative process done through the MBC-INAAN courts

14. Are there official marriages/divorces/etc.?

Yes.

MBC-INAAN CODE ANNOTATED:

Title 1, § 2–110. Solemnization of marriages

Ceremony. All marriages must be contracted by a formal ceremony performed or solemnized in the presence of at least two (2) adult, competent persons as witnesses, by a judge or retired judge of any Court of the MBC-INAAN, or an ordained or authorized preacher or minister of the Gospel, priest or other ecclesiastical dignitary of any denomination who has been duly ordained or authorized by the church to which he or she belongs to preach the Gospel, and who is at least eighteen (18) years of age; by a person commissioned by the Appellate Judge after a proper application and examination; or by the clan elder in the case of a marriage solemnized at a ceremonial ground.

15. Is this an Islamic, Christian, Hebrew, Buddhist, Nuwaubian/Sabean organization?

No. This is an Indigenous Native American Government for indigenous people(s).

The Mund Bareefan Clan (of House Thunderbird) is the indigenous clan/tribe/family, that established and made the Non-Religious MBC-INAAN Government.

There may be individuals that belong to various religious, civic or social organizations, that may be nationals of our Association of Nations. This does not refer to their nationalization.

16. Are Moors/Muurs or other aboriginal or indigenous peoples welcome?

Mund Bareefan Clan is a specific Guale/Yamassee Clan. MBC-INAAN agencies provide services to indigenous and aboriginal peoples with no discrimination.

17. Must one belong to a clan to receive services from MBC-INAAN?

We provide services to indigenous and aboriginal peoples, and indigenous and aboriginal individuals through the Indigenous Native American Recording Service (INARS) in accord with our laws; and in accord with international laws relating to cultural, social and governmental practices for indigenous peoples.

MBC-INAAN Constitution Bill of Rights, Article 35

MBC-INAAN People, in particular those divided by international borders, have the right to maintain and develop contacts, relations and cooperation, including activities for spiritual, cultural, political, economic and social purposes, **with other peoples across borders. States shall take effective measures to ensure the exercise and implementation of this right.**

United Nations Declaration on the Rights of Indigenous Peoples, Article 36

Indigenous peoples, in particular those divided by international borders, have the right to maintain and develop contacts, relations and cooperation, including activities for spiritual, cultural, political, economic and social purposes, with their own members as well as other peoples across borders.

States, in consultation and cooperation with indigenous peoples, shall take effective measures to facilitate the exercise and ensure the implementation of this right.

18. Is religion a determination to your nationality?

With the MBC-INAAN, nationality is a secular/non-religious conscious decision of an adult, should not be coerced.

Over time indigenous people have embraced many religions, fraternal, and civic interest. We use ethnic and religious titles like Negro, Black American, Chicano, Latino American, Moorish American, Nuwaubian, African American, Muslim, Ansar, Christian, and there are others.

These are good honorable things to be. Some of these titles we consider national/international designations as autonomous. They are not. None of the above titles gives you international recognition as Autonomous Indigenous Peoples in the United States.

19. Does your clan have a religion or faith?

Concerning the people of the MBC proper, we live what is called Reflective Human Socialization. We honor and are grateful to all of the Masters and their teachings.

Concerning the people of the MBC-INAAN as Individuals, we continue in our chosen faiths.

Jointly, we exist as indigenous peoples we are". We lay claim, that we are indigenous peoples with personal, historical, State, and US Federal Acknowledgement of our birth rights as the indigenous peoples we are.

20. What is House Royal Thunderbird ?

House Royal Thunderbird is the **Mund Bareefan Embassy Clan**.

The "Most Principal Chief and Chief Executive of the "Guale/Yamassee" is the Guale Chief, Chief Black-Hawk H. Thunderbird, of the "Mund Bareefan Embassy Clan" which is of the Guale Chiefdom. The founding Clan/family of the Yamassee Union of 1992 is the "La Tama Clan" (Ta Ma Re) of Grand Chief Black Thunderbird Eagle;

The two principal families of these clans are family, "blood and mud in fact." Together we are "House Thunderbird" also called "Royal Thunderbird". The "Most Principal Chief; and Chief Executive of our

Association of Nations, is the Guale Chief, Chief Black-Hawk H. Thunderbird, of the "Mund Bareefan Embassy Clan". With regard to our internal and local affairs, all of this falls under the legal jurisdiction of the Guale Chiefdom.

With the participation of other associated indigenous tribes, families and indigenous individuals we are the "Mund Bareefan Embassy Clan/Indigenous Native American Association of Nations" (MBC/INAAN).

Our Association is established, Authenticated, and is Acknowledged by ourselves, as well as Federally and in the sevel States of the United States of America.

21. Are there elections in the MBC-INAAN?

Yes.

MBC-INAAN Constitution Article 18

Section 5: When There Are Openings:

> When There Are Openings in Representation from Any Gabelu, Or an

Official Is Dis-fellowshipped, The Opening Shall Be Filled Immediately by Way of Election of Governing High Council.

TITLE 19, § 4–101.persons entitled to vote in Tribal elections

> Every person who is a qualified National of the MBC-INAAN according to the Constitution of the MBC-INAAN, regardless of religion, creed, or sex, shall be eligible to vote in the Tribal elections...

22. Are natives of surrounding Islands welcome?

INAAN agencies provide services to indigenous and aboriginal peoples. Mund Bareefan Clan is a specific clan and makers of the MBC-INAAN. We provide services to indigenous peoples and individuals in accord with our laws and international laws relating to cultural, social and governmental practices of indigenous people.

MBC-INAAN Constitution Bill of Rights, Article 35

MBC-INAAN People, in particular those divided by international borders, have the right to maintain and develop contacts, relations and cooperation, including activities for spiritual, cultural, political, economic and social purposes, **with other peoples across borders. States shall take effective measures to ensure the exercise and implementation of this right.**

United Nations Declaration on the Rights of Indigenous Peoples, Article 36

Indigenous peoples, in particular those divided by international borders, have the right to maintain and develop contacts, relations and cooperation, including activities for spiritual, cultural, political, economic and social purposes, with their own members as well as other peoples across borders. States, in consultation and cooperation with indigenous peoples, shall take effective measures to facilitate the exercise and ensure the implementation of this right.

23. Do we pay taxes? Child support?

Yes, and yes.

24. Do we have to move anywhere?

No.

ABOUT MBC-INAAN CHILDREN

25. What does indigenous mean to our children?

The of MBC-INAAN society shall be centered around the well-being of the children, our posterity. It is our responsibility to provide peaceful harmonious well-balanced environments for our children: this will also will be beneficial to all within our jurisdictions.

MBC-INAAN Constitution, Article 3: PEACE

§ Section 3. We the People MBC-INAAN must change the condition in our mind, in order to live in harmonious, well-balanced, stable, peaceful environments. We have to change the course of our lives for the better, which will change the way our children Are being programmed. We must create environments suitable and protective.

26. What is MBC-INAAN position on education, should our children participate in the educational systems of the local governments?

We live in the rapid information, High- Tech-knowledge Era. It is paramount that we make educational, medical, technical, and industrial institutions that will prepare our children to thrive in this new world.

We should be prepared to use all forms of Tech-Knowledge, science and medicine. This means that we should participate with other educational institutions for the sake of our advancement.

By preparing for the children, we also prepare for the elders and the able-bodied adults and young people of our Chiefdom.

MBC-INAAN Constitution, Article 14: EDUCATION

> § Section 5. The Imparting of General Knowledge and Skills That Will Help the Children of Mund Bareefan Clan-Indigenous Native American Association of Nations Participate Fully and on an Equal Footing Shall Be an Aim of Education For MBC-INAAN Peoples.

27. What happens if a local government child enforcement agency files a complaint against an MBC-INAAN family/child?

All jurisdiction of MBC-INAAN children is under the protection of the laws of the MBC-INAAN Child Welfare Law. You should contact your local clan mothers and a "GAR" Attorney for assistance with all matters concerning MBC-INAAN family and children.

MBC-INAAN Constitution, Article 2: JUSTICE

We the People MBC-INAAN Hereby
Declare Our Right to Self-Determination,
The Right to Autonomy, Or Self-
Government in Matters Relating to Our
Internal and Local Affairs Including
Culture, Religion, Information, Education,
Media, Health, Housing, Employment,
Social Welfare, Economic Activity, Land
And Resource Management,
Environment, Financial Security, and
Welfare.

Excerpts from the "Brief in Support" section of the
binding Constructive International "Agreement" of
Feb. 11th, 2004, between the USA and the Mund
Bareefan Clan via the US Department of State.

The of Bill of Rights Of MBC/INAA Constitution, Article
31

Indigenous people, as a specific form of
exercising their right to self-
determination, have the right to

autonomy or self-government in matters relating to their internal and local affairs, including culture, religion, education, welfare, economics activities, land and resourced, management, environment and entry by non-members, as well as ways and means for financing these autonomous functions.

The of Bill of Rights Of MBC-INAAN Indigenous Peoples, Article 36

Indigenous people have the right to the recognition, observance and enforcement of treaties, agreements and other constructive arrangements concluded with States or their successor, according to their original sprit of intent, and to have States' honor and respect such treaties, agreements and other constructive arrangements. Conflicts and disputes which cannot otherwise be settled should be submitted to competent international bodies agreed to by all parties concerned...

This international agreement is protected by MBC-INAAN CA, Title 29: chapter 1 Section 116:

The edition of the laws and treaties of the MBC-INAAN, published by Mund Bareefan, and the publications in slip or pamphlet form of the laws of the MBC-INAAN, issued under the authority of the Archivist of the MBC-INAAN, and the Treaties and Other International Acts Series issued under the authority of the Supreme Grand Chief or the Principal Grand Chiefs, shall be competent evidence of the several public and private Acts of The Governing High Council, the treaties, international agreements other than treaties, and proclamations by the Supreme Grand Chief of such treaties and international agreements other than treaties, as the case may be, therein contained, in all the courts of law and equity and of maritime jurisdiction, and in all the tribunals and public offices of the MBC-INAAN, and of the sevel Clans/tribes, without any further proof or authentication thereof.

All non-judicial records or books kept in any public office of any Clan, Territory, or Possession of the MBC-INAAN, or copies thereof, shall be proved or admitted in any court or office in any other Clan, Territory, or Possession by the attestation of the custodian of such records or books, and the seal of his office annexed, if there be a seal, together with a certificate of a judge of a court of record of the county, parish, or district in which such office may be kept, or of the Chief, or secretary of state, the chancellor or keeper of the great seal, of the Clan, Territory, or Possession that the said attestation is in due form and by the proper officers.

The USC ANNOTATED: Title 1 chapter 2 section 113. Is similar.

The edition of the laws and treaties of the United States, published by Little and Brown, and the publications in slip or pamphlet form of the laws of the United States issued under the authority of the Archivist of the United States, and the Treaties and Other International Acts Series issued under the authority of the Secretary of State shall be competent evidence of the several public and private Acts of Congress, and of the treaties, international agreements other than treaties, and proclamations by the President of such treaties and international agreements other than treaties, as the case may be, therein contained, in all the courts of law and equity and of maritime jurisdiction, and in all the tribunals and public offices of the United States, and of the sevel States, without any further proof or authentication thereof.

All non-judicial records or books kept in any public office of any State, Territory, or Possession of the United States, or copies thereof, shall be proved or admitted in any court or office in any other State, Territory, or Possession by the attestation of the custodian of such records or books, and the seal of his office annexed, if there be a seal, together with a certificate of a judge of a court of record of the county, parish, or district in which such office may be kept, or of the Governor, or secretary of state, the chancellor or keeper of the great seal, of the State, Territory, or Possession that the said attestation is in due form and by the proper officers.

Well, as they say on Saturday Night Live: "Talk about amongst yourselves.   I'll give you a topic". **"Indigenous Self-determination" v. "Sovereignty".**

Unity   **Individualism**

CONCLUSION

Gesur Black-Hawk H. Thunderbird aka "Sage Ramus" in the "Society of Geography and Statistics" in Mexico City, in 2011 speaking at the invitation of the Mexican Senate.

We must be viewed with hopes, and act with cooperation with each other and with others. We should harbor spiritual thought that reties all humans together. We are to affirm that there is no longer man, neither woman, neither slave, neither liberal, neither conservative, neither I, Miss, Mr., or national, we all are one in the species human of earth; and this alliance should be reformed in the context of planetary civilization. There is no longer neither white nor black, neither native neither migrant, neither Westerner, neither Asian, neither believer neither non-believer. On this planet, we all have the same civic responsibilities.

IN

LOVING MEMORY

OF

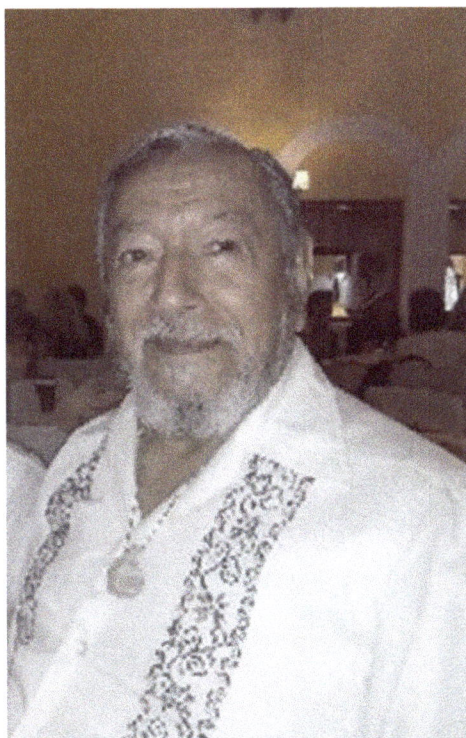

Dr. Raymundo Lopez Ortiz
09/2021

www.ingramcontent.com/pod-product-compliance
Lightning Source LLC
Chambersburg PA
CBHW071132280326
41935CB00010B/1194